Hmm, So You Have A Problem Workbook

HMM, SO YOU HAVE A PROBLEM WORKBOOK

Biblical Answers to Everyday Situations

by Mary Cullinane

COPYRIGHT © 2016

Hmm, So You Have A Problem Workbook

Chapter	Title	Page
1	Depression Can be Cured	3
2	Root of Drug and Alcohol Addiction	7
3	satan's Curse – Drugs	11
4	One Day at a Time	16
5	Be Anxious for Nothing	19
6	Insecurity – Low Self-Esteem	22
7	Fear-False Events Appear to be Real	26
8	Despair – Let's Not Give Into It	29
9	Contentment, Peace, and Harmony	32
10	Betrayal – the Unexpected	36
11	How Can We Handle Rejection?	39
12	Familiarity Breeds Contempt	42
13	Forgiveness – A Difficult Virtue	45
14	How to Regain Trust	49
15	Lack of Commitment	52
16	Don't Delay – Just Do It!	55
17	Inspiration–Where Does It Come From?	58
18	Impulsive Behavior Gets Us In Trouble	61
19	Wisdom of Solomon	64
20	Pride – The Insidious Emotion	67
21	Anger Can Kill	72
22	I Don't Get Mad, I Get Even	75
23	Hate Can Destroy	78
24	Control – The Suffocator	81
25	A Gentle Answer	84
26	Dual Personality – How Prevalent	87
27	Love is Not Receiving, It is Giving	91
28	Husbands Love Your Wives	94
29	Overcoming Sexual Problems	97
30	Why Do We Limit God in Our Lives?	100
31	Is Your Faith Real?	103
32	Am I Doing God a Favor?	106
33	Adoption – Perhaps the Best Mothers	109
	Epilogue – Tying It All Together	112

Hmm, So You Have A Problem Workbook

Chapter 1

DEPRESSION CAN BE CURED

Then Jesus said to His disciples, "That's why I'm telling you to stop worrying about your life-what you will eat-or about your body-what you will wear. For life is more than food and the body more than clothing." Luke 12:22-23

The word *life* used in Luke chapter 12 is *psuche* in the Greek, like psyche. I am convinced from observation that the people who are mentally unbalanced or depressed are always thinking about themselves. They go over and over all the hurts they have experienced and in so doing, make matters much worse. Our enemy, satan, is more than pleased to add fuel to the fire of discontent. So Jesus gave us an antidote - stop thinking about ourselves!

Ever since psychology became the rage, people have been having many more mental problems. It seems that people have labels for so many of their problems because of over-analyzing their lives. Jesus and time will heal any wounds. Can't we trust Him?

For life is more than food and the body more than clothing. Jesus continued: *Consider the crows. They don't plant or harvest, they don't even have a storeroom or barn, yet God feeds them. How much more valuable are you than birds!* Luke 12:24

Consider the crows. You don't see depressed birds flying around. They are busy! They provide nests for their young and they provide food for themselves and their young. Why don't we take an example from the birds and stay busy for others and in so doing, we probably would not become depressed. We can learn from God's creations. Jesus also said: *Can any of you add an hour to your span of life by worrying?* Luke 12:25

Can we, by thinking about ourselves, make ourselves taller? If we are overweight, the best way to trim down is to get busy and stop thinking about what we will eat. Can we add to our life span by worrying about getting older? Getting older causes depression for quite a few people. Maybe one of the reasons is that we are such a youth oriented country. The only alternative that I see to growing older is to die young. So, let us rejoice that the Lord has granted us a long life that we may enjoy our grandchildren and the fruit of our labors.

Why don't we become more than the way we look? When the bloom of youth fades, there should be something left, which is goodness, peace, wisdom, and holiness. Peter said: *Your beauty should not be an external one, consisting of braided hair or the wearing of gold ornaments and dresses. Instead, it should be the inner disposition of the heart, consisting in the imperishable quality of a gentle and quiet spirit, which is of great value in the sight of God.* 1Pe 3:3-4

Dear Paul told us: *Never worry about anything, but in every situation let your petitions be made known to God in prayers and requests, with thanksgiving. Then God's peace, which goes far beyond anything we can imagine, will guard your hearts and minds in Christ Jesus.*

Finally, brothers, whatever is true, whatever is honorable, whatever is fair, whatever is pure, whatever is acceptable, whatever is commendable, if there is anything of excellence and if there is anything praiseworthy-keep thinking about these things. Philippians 4:6-8

So we are told never to worry about anything. The word *worry* in the Greek (New Testament was written first in the Greek language) means to be careful, take thought or to be anxious. Jesus will free us from all anxiety if we call on Him and lean on Him. He promised us: *And you will know the truth and the truth will set you free.* John 8:32. Free is free, right? If Jesus sets us free, He does not set us half free; He sets us totally free.

He also exhorted us: *Consider how the lilies grow. They don't work or spin yarn, but I tell you that not even Solomon in all his splendor was clothed like one of them. Now if that's the way God clothes the grass in the field, which is alive today and thrown into an oven tomorrow, how much more will he clothe you-you who have little faith? So stop concerning yourselves* doubtful *about what you will eat or what you will drink, and stop being distressed.* Luke 12:27-29

Hmm, So You Have A Problem Workbook

Stop being distressed or of a doubtful mind. The words *doubtful mind* mean raised in mid air - that is suspended - to fluctuate or be anxious. That makes us vacillate from one opinion to another.

Jesus told us: *...I am the way, the truth, and the life. No one comes to the Father except through me.* John 14:6. So the closer we get to Jesus, through prayer, the Word, praise and worship, the less doubts we will have about life and eternity.

Again He said: *For it is the gentiles who are concerned about all these things. Surely your Father knows that you need them! Instead, be concerned about his kingdom, and these things will be provided for you as well.* Luke 12:30-31. By gentiles He means the people who are pagans, who don't know God. *Concerned* in this case means to seek after, desire, or be about.

So if the simple things of life, like flowers and birds and sunsets are so beautiful, why don't we just enjoy them as a gift from God and enjoy life as a gift from God, and try to be the person that He created us to be? If we stay concerned about the things of God, we are more likely not to become depressed, anxious, or worried. Our minds and thoughts will be way above those petty things in life that formerly got us down. Try it! Every time you feel as if you are getting depressed or blue, say a prayer to Jesus and ask Him to loose your burden. Our prayers won't fail because He never fails!

Hmm, So You Have A Problem Workbook

Questions:

1. _____ is more than _____ and the body more than _____.
2. Psychology labels problems but does not always _____ our problems.
3. *How much more valuable are you than _____ but your heavenly Father takes care of them.*
4. *Can any of you add an hour to your span of _____?*
5. _____ said *your beauty should not be an external one.*
6. Paul tells us _____ worry about anything.
7. _____ is to take thought, to be careful or anxious.
8. _____ can set us free.
9. What does raised in mid air mean? _____
10. Who *is the way, the truth and the life?* _____
11. The closer we get to Jesus through _____, _____, _____, the less doubts we will have about life and eternity.

Discuss how you have overcome anxieties and fears.

Chapter 2

ROOT OF DRUG AND ALCOHOL ADDICTION

...the garment of praise for the spirit of heaviness... Isaiah 61:3 ASV)

One of the inmates from the county jail had written to me asking for help in understanding her depression and also had questions about generational curses. I had planned to teach something else. Instead I started to talk to my group about depression. I teach three classes on Sunday mornings. At each class I asked if the women were depressed before becoming addicted to drugs - *every hand went up*! So I felt we were on to something!

Have you heard about King Asa? In 2Chronicles chapter 15 we read that the Spirit of God came upon Azariah to prophesy to King Asa that he and all of Judah and Benjamin were not living the lives they should and that there must be repentance in the entire land. So King Asa harkened to the prophet and cleansed the land. He destroyed all the idols the people had worshiped and renewed the places of worship. (This must have taken a good deal of time, probably years.) Then he assembled all the people at Jerusalem and they brought sacrifices for the Lord which were 700 oxen and 7000 sheep. (Now in those days, there were no cowboys, so to assemble that many animals must have taken a lot of time also.) The people swore an oath to worship the Lord with all their hearts and souls. Then now we come to the 16th verse.

And also Maacah, the mother of Asa the king, he removed from being queen, because she had made an abominable image for an Asherah; and Asa cut down her image, and made dust of it, and burnt it at the brook Kidron 2Chronicles 15:16

Maacah was the grandmother of King Asa (called mother in Chronicles). What is so significant about this is that the name Maacah means *depression or oppression*! It was a long time before King Asa realized that there was idol worship in his own house! Grandmothers are very familiar to us - we hardly notice they are around. Familiar spirits are like that too. We may have experienced the spirit of depression from the time we were very young and thus do not realize that it is still around. A person doesn't usually wake up and feel depressed after going to bed in a happy mood - it is a gradual process and finally the person is so down that he cannot see his way out.

My women at the jail had all felt depressed before giving in to drug addiction. The drugs seemed a way out, but of course, they only made matters much worse. So a light went on in my head that if the spirit of depression was removed from the women's lives, the spirit of drugs might also be annihilated!

So then I looked to Isaiah: *To appoint unto them that mourn in Zion, to give unto them beauty for ashes, the oil of joy for mourning, the garment of praise for the spirit of heaviness; that they might be called trees of righteousness, the planting of the LORD, that he might be glorified.* Isaiah 61:3

The garment of praise for the spirit of heaviness! God promised us that praise will eliminate the spirit of heaviness!! When we start to praise the Lord, the enemy has to leave. He cannot stay where the praises of the Lord are being sung. This explains why so many people feel good while at church and then fall away when they leave. We should develop the joy of praising the Lord at all times. If we do, we can chase the spirit of heaviness or depression away!

Can you agree with me that praise is an antidote to drug addiction? We should also remain busy serving the Lord and helping people, and then we will not easily sink into the morass of depression. As is said in 1Corinthians chapter 12, there is a gift of the Holy Spirit which is discernment of spirits. Ask the Lord to give you that gift and when the familiar spirit of heaviness or depression starts to come upon you, start to praise the Lord. If it still persists, call a Christian sister or brother to pray and agree with you.

Jesus said: *Verily I say unto you, Whatsoever ye shall bind on earth shall be bound in heaven: and whatsoever ye shall loose on earth shall be loosed in heaven. Again I say unto you, That if two of you shall agree on earth as touching any thing that they shall ask, it shall be done for them of my Father which is in heaven.* Matthew 18:18-19

Jesus told us that we can bind the spirit of depression and all of

Hmm, So You Have A Problem Workbook

Heaven will be in agreement with us. He said that if we agree with another Christian sister or brother, then it shall be done for us by our Father Who is in Heaven. This is powerful and very easy to understand. If we do not allow the spirit of depression to come in, we will not have to deal with the spirit of drugs. Think of it! Drug addicts or alcoholics are not happy, peaceful people. They often are sad and depressed and this is the precursor to addiction. Then they turn to a substance which they think will help to get out of their unpleasant states and that only makes matters worse.

Matthew chapter 12 talked about ...*binding the strong man*. If the strong man of depression is bound in our lives, our houses will be safe and not invaded by a lot of other bad spirits.

So let us right now bind the spirit of depression in the Name of Jesus, so that it will no longer have a stronghold in our lives. And let us pray right now for discernment of the spirit of heaviness or depression. If we do discern it around us, ask God to give us the wisdom to praise Him for all the wonderful things He does in our lives. The spirit of heaviness must leave when we put on the garment of praise!

Hmm, So You Have A Problem Workbook

Questions:

1. _____ oftentimes precedes drug abuse.
2. _____ King Asa's grandmother means _____ or _____.
3. Grandmothers can be likened to _____ spirits as we are so used to having them around that we do not notice them.
4. Depression is usually a _____ problem.
5. Drugs seem to be a way out but they only make _____ worse.
6. Isaiah said *the garment of _____ for the spirit of heaviness*.
7. When we start to praise the Lord what has to leave? _____
8. The gift of _____ of spirits will aid us in discovering when we are sinking into depression and we can ask the Lord to rid us of that spirit.
9. And whom can we agree with here on earth to rid us of that spirit? _____
10. If the strong man of _____ is bound in our lives, our houses will be safe.

Discuss how the spirit of depression has left when we put on the garments of praise.

Chapter 3

SATAN'S CURSE - DRUGS

And you will know the truth, and the truth will set you free. John 8:32

While teaching Bible studies at the county jail, I wondered why so many nice women were there because of drug addiction. When the drugs are removed, they become sweet, honest, mothers concerned with their children and families, and responsive to the Word of God. So I looked to the Word for the answer.

Jesus said: *The person who conquers will inherit these things. I will be his God, and he will be my son. But people who are cowardly, unfaithful, detestable, murderers, sexually immoral, sorcerers, idolaters, and all liars will find themselves in the lake that burns with fire and sulfur. This is the second death.* Revelation 21:7-8

The word *sorcerers* in verse 8 is *pharmakeia* in the Greek which means enchantment with drugs. There is witchcraft involved in drug use, so this may explain the power drugs have over a person's life.

Paul said: *And no wonder, since satan himself masquerades as an angel of light.* 2Corinthians 11:14

Angel dust?

John prophesied: *...and all the nations were deceived by your witchcraft.* Revelation 18:23 Nations in the Greek is *ethnos* - ethnic groups rather than geographical areas as we perceive nations. There are no cultural distinctions when practicing drug abuse. People who are living a *low life* are approached for drugs by people who would ordinarily have nothing to do with them (dealers). The enchantment with drugs deceives all - rich and poor, good upbringing, street upbringing. It is a way that satan uses to deceive people. *Deceive* in the Greek means to go astray, seduce, wander, be out of the way.

Jesus warned us: *The thief comes only to steal, slaughter, and destroy. I have come that they may have life, and have it abundantly.* John 10:10 Think about it. Satan takes over when we yield to drugs and then what? He steals our possessions, especially families; he kills our relationships with others; often causes us to commit crimes of violence; and then he destroys our relationships, health, and families. Remember, the first time drugs are offered, they are *free*. After that, it's pay, pay, pay!

The word *substance* in the Greek means strength, calamity, wealth, force, might, existence, power, acquisition, goods, wisdom, being. Is it any wonder that drug abuse is called substance abuse? What is lost when we give our bodies to satan during drug abuse? Satan controls our wealth, strength, power, acquisitions, goods, and our whole beings.

Paul told us: *…so that, just as sin ruled by bringing death, so also grace might rule by bringing justification that results in eternal life through Jesus Christ our Lord.* Romans 5:21

There is a solution to drug abuse and that Solution is Jesus Christ! Jesus gave us the promise: *So if the Son sets you free, you will be free indeed!* John 8:36

Paul said: *Therefore, through baptism we were buried with him into his death so that, just as Christ was raised from the dead by the Father's glory, we too may live an entirely new life.* Romans 6:4. *The person who has died has been freed from sin. Now if we have died with Christ, we believe that we will also live with him.* Romans 6:7-8 *Therefore, if anyone is in Christ, he is a new creation. Old things have disappeared, and-look!-all things have become new!* 2Corinthians 5:17

We can live a new, free life when we give our hearts to Jesus and let Him be the Lord of our lives. But Solomon warned us: *He who digs a pit shall fall into it; and whoever breaks a hedge, a snake shall bite him.* Ecclesiastes 10:8

Complaining about Job to God, satan said, *"Have You not made a hedge about him …"* Job 1:10

We see from the Scriptures that when we give our hearts to the Lord, He builds a hedge of protection around us. However, when we introduce illicit drugs into our systems, we are the ones who break our hedges and then the serpent (devil) has the right to bite us. The enemy always loves to get us to do something wrong and then when we do, he

Hmm, So You Have A Problem Workbook

laughs at us.

The writer of Proverbs rightly described the sadness of addiction: *Who has woe? Who has sorrow? Who has fighting? Who has babbling? Who has wounds without cause? Who has redness of eyes? Those who stay long at the wine, those who go to seek mixed wine. Do not look upon the wine when it is red, when it gives its color in the cup, when it goes down smoothly. At the last it bites like an asp and stings like an adder. Your eyes shall look upon strange women and your heart shall speak perverse things. Yes, you shall be as one who lies down in the middle of the sea, or as one who lies upon the top of a mast, saying, They struck me; I was not sick; they beat me, but I did not know it. When I awaken, I will add more. I will seek it again.* Proverbs 23:29-35

Jesus gave us a solution when He said: *...Whatever you shall bind on earth shall occur, having been bound in Heaven; and whatever you shall loose on earth shall occur, having been loosed in Heaven.* Matthew 18:18 So if we pray in the name of Jesus to bind the spirit of drugs and witchcraft in our lives, He will loose us from the treachery that is involved in drug addiction.

Right now, will you pray with me? Heavenly Father, I come before you in the Name of Jesus. I know that Jesus died on the cross for all my sins and that He rose from the dead and that He is God. I ask you Jesus, to forgive all my sins, and I bind satan and all his evil works in Your Holy Name, Jesus. I rebuke satan and all his works. I ask You Jesus to forgive all my sins, to come into my heart and life, and to be my Lord and Savior all the days of my life. In your Holy Name Jesus, Amen.

In order to live free from drugs and sin:

1. Pray every day.
2. Read your Bible - it is God's love letter to you.
3. Stay away from people, places, and music that have caused you to stray.
4. Go to a Bible believing church. A good criterion includes a church where people take their Bibles. There will be those there who are more experienced in the ways of life and the wiles of the enemy

and who can help you resist trials and temptations.

5. Try to associate with other people who love the Lord and have overcome the enemy.

6. Stay away from alcohol. That, too, is a drug.

7. Thank God every day for your deliverance from the curse of drug abuse.

8. Realize that it is the grace of God that keeps you from alcohol or drug abuse.

Recovering alcoholics and drug abusers have a sign in their meetings that says "but for the grace of God." It's a great reminder that each day we can overcome the enemy only by the grace of God. When we think we can do it our way, by our set of rules, we are in danger of a fall. But when we realize that only by the grace of God have we come this far, we will be able to overcome all that the world is pleased to hurl at us.

So let's pray right now to be humble and receive grace from God to persevere in our faith and to be fulfilled in Jesus.

Hmm, So You Have A Problem Workbook

Questions:

1. *And you will know the truth and the _____ will set you _____.* John 8:32
2. The word sorcery in the New Testament Greek means enchantment with _____.
3. *Ethnos* in the NT means _____.
4. _____ means to go astray, seduce, wander, be out of the way.
5. Who is the great deceiver? _____
6. Who comes to steal, slaughter and destroy? _____
7. What does he oftentimes use to do all that? _____
8. The first time drugs are offered, they are usually _____.
9. Afterward it is _____ _____ _____.
10. The word _____ in the Greek means strength, calamity, wealth, force, might, existence, power, acquisition, goods, wisdom, being.
11. _____ abuse is what addiction to drugs is called.
12. Who is the solution to drug abuse? _____ _____
13. *So if the _____ sets you free, you will be _____ indeed.*
14. *Therefore if anyone is in _____, he is a new creation. Old things have disappeared and -look!-all things have become new!* 2Corinthaians 5:17
15. When we give our hearts to God, He puts a _____ of protection around us.
16. Who or what will remove that hedge? _____
17. *Who has woe? Who has sorrow?* The _____ addict.

Discuss some of the ways we can stay free from drugs and sin.

Hmm, So You Have A Problem Workbook

Chapter 4

ONE DAY AT A TIME

Give us this day our daily bread... Matthew 6:11

How many of us live in the past or in the future? Someone said that the present is a present. Let's not miss out on it! When Jesus was at Bethany in Simon the leper's house, shortly before His death on the cross, a woman anointed Him with a very costly spikenard. When she did, she broke open the bottle showing her complete abandonment to the Lord. Some of the apostles, especially Judas, upbraided her for wasting the ointment. But Jesus said, *"Leave her alone. Why are you bothering her? She has done a beautiful thing for me. For you will always have the destitute with you and can help them whenever you want, but you will not always have me. She has done what she could. She poured perfume on my body in preparation for my burial."* Mark 14:6-8

"She has done what she could!" This is a key to an open Heaven for us. If we do the best we can, when we can, Heaven is open to us. God does not expect us to do beyond that which He has given us the grace to do. Some people say to me, "How can you go into the prisons, aren't you afraid?" I usually reply, "It's like meeting women on the beach and talking with them." Why? Because God has given me the grace to do that which I can and not worry about it. It's enjoyable if you are doing what the Lord gives you the grace to do. I don't worry about tomorrow - I am just happy today.

What hold do we have on tomorrow? What guarantees do we have? None! So why not enjoy the present as a *present*? How many plans have we had that went awry? The Lord does want us to provide financially for our old age, but we can get so caught up in worrying about money that we do not enjoy our present blessings.

Did you hear about the stingy man who would not let his wife have any of his money? He made her promise that she would get all his money together and put it in his coffin if he died first. Well, he did die first. At the funeral, she put a box in his casket. Her friend said to her, "Why are you doing that? You are not giving him all that money to bury with him, are you?" The widow replied, "I am a Christian and I made a promise to him. I researched all of his money and wrote him a check. If he can cash it, it's his!"

Let's say a prayer right now to lighten up and appreciate our present life. This moment is all that we have with certainty.

Hmm, So You Have A Problem Workbook

Questions:

1. When the woman anointed Jesus with a very costly spikenard at Simon the leper's house, she showed complete _____ to the Lord.
2. She had done what she _____.
3. If we do the best we can, when we can, _____ is open to us.
4. _____ does not expect us to do beyond that which He has given us the grace to do.

Discuss how we have enjoyed our day today without worrying about the future.

Hmm, So You Have A Problem Workbook

Chapter 5

BE ANXIOUS FOR NOTHING

In nothing be anxious; but in everything by prayer and supplication with thanksgiving let your requests be made known unto God. Philippians 4:6

The word anxious, the root word anxiety, comes from the Latin word angere which means to choke. What an appropriate description of the feelings of anxiety! To choke is used in sports terms when a person is up against a tough situation and just cannot seem to come through. If we are all choked up in life, we certainly are not living life to the fullest or even enjoying life. Let's examine what causes anxiety and why some people suffer from it and others don't.

Does our happiness depend upon worldly possessions? From my observations, no. I have seen people who own many possessions who suffer from anxiety and I have seen other people who are old and live from day to day and have very few worldly possessions who are happy and content. The apostle Paul had a handle on this when he said: *For the love of money is a root of all kinds of evil: which some reaching after have been led astray from the faith, and have pierced themselves through with many sorrows.* 1Timothy 6:10

Is money the root of all evil? We sometimes hear that, but Paul said that the *love* of money is the root of all evil. We can be rich and not love money and we can be poor and love money. So we see that having possessions or not having possessions is not the root of the problem of anxiety.

Let's examine another situation that could be the cause of anxiety - fear of getting old. What is there to fear when we approach old age? Is it loss of health, loss of beauty, and especially, loss of life? Could we be feeling anxiety because we have a fear of death? It seems very plausible.

To *choke up* on a situation means that we do not have any control over it. For example, if the call is three balls and two strikes against the baseball batter, and there are two outs in the ninth inning and this would be the tying run, the man at bat may indeed choke up as the pressure of the situation overwhelms him.

So to, when we are facing the reality of death, the pressure of the unknown may cause us to choke up. What is the antidote for fear of death? The apostle John told us: *There is no fear where love exists. Rather, perfect love banishes fear, for fear involves punishment, and the person who lives in fear has not been perfected in love.* 1John 4:18 John also said: *We love because God loved us first.* 1John 4:19

So let us pray to receive the love that God is willing to bestow upon us. The more love we have from and for God, the more our anxieties will be choked out.

Hmm, So You Have A Problem Workbook

Questions:

1. What does anxious mean? ___ _____
2. Does our happiness depend on worldly things? _____
3. *For the* _____ *of money is a root of all kinds of evil.*
4. Could we be feeling anxiety because of a fear of _____?
5. To choke up on a situation means that we do not have _____ over it.
6. What is the antidote for fear? _____
7. The apostle John told us that *perfect* _____ *banishes fear.*
8. The person who lives in fear has not been perfected in _____.
9. The more love we have from and for God, the more our anxieties will be _____ _____

Discuss how the love of God in you has kept you from being anxious about things.

Hmm, So You Have A Problem Workbook

Chapter 6

INSECURITY - LOW SELF-ESTEEM

You created every part of me; you put me together in my mother's womb. Psalm 139:13

I'm too fat. I'm too skinny. I'm too tall. I'm too short. I'm too fair. I'm too dark. Don't we get tired of thinking those thoughts? Who created us that we are so critical of ourselves? *So God created human beings, making them to be like himself. He created them male and female.* Genesis 1:27

Why are we so critical of God's creation? The Psalmist said: *You created every part of me; you put me together in my mother's womb. I praise you because you are to be feared; all you do is strange and wonderful. I know it with all my heart. When my bones were being formed, carefully put together in my mother's womb, when I was growing there in secret, you knew that I was there--- you saw me before I was born. The days allotted to me had all been recorded in your book, before any of them ever began.* Psalm 139:13-16

If God chose to create us tall or short, fair or dark, why do we dwell on that which we are not? Fat or thin can be determined by diet and exercise later, but our original bodies were determined while in our mother's womb.

When the scribes asked Jesus what was the foremost commandment of all, Jesus replied, *"The most important one is this: 'Listen, Israel! The Lord our God is the only Lord. Love the Lord your God with all your heart, with all your soul, with all your mind, and with all your strength.' The second most important commandment is this: 'Love your neighbor as you love yourself.' There is no other commandment more important than these two."* Mark 12:29-31

Jesus told us to love our neighbor (fellow man), as ourselves. So He told us to love ourselves! To have the same regard for ourselves as we have for another person. It's not conceit to love ourselves and to think well of ourselves if we love God first. If we love God first, we will realize we are lovable in His eyes. If we can always sustain that realization, we should never think badly of ourselves again.

Many people who think down on themselves have established impossible goals. If we realize our capabilities in our present situations, we will try to fulfill them and not become discouraged when we fall short, instead we will try harder the next time.

When my granddaughter was 10 years old, she decided to play ice hockey. It was offered at her small school. At tryouts, as she had only skated twice in her life, she was pretty bad. She couldn't skate backwards, she was uneven, and really made a bad appearance. After the tryouts, she skated to her mom and dad, took off her helmet, steam coming out of her head she said, "I wasn't that bad, right?" She went on to skate for the next three years, facing serious competition. Had she been only aware of her shortcomings on the first trial, she probably never would have made it. She may have given up. However, she had confidence that she could make it and she did!

About the same time her grandmother (me) started to play tennis at age 65! Hadn't played since I was about 15 years old. I took lessons, read books and played as often as I could find partners. After a while, I could play with serious players. I felt great about it. I didn't groan or get angry with myself when I didn't make some shots, and after the game, I remembered my good plays. So the game is fun for me as I have not set impossible goals for myself. I will never go pro! Too late for that. With my friends, I am considered good, and I also consider myself good! So should there be more? I don't think so. I don't receive criticism on things that do not mean anything such as games. Games should be played for fun unless, of course, if you are a pro. But even pros seem to do better in a relaxed atmosphere rather than a tense one. So if you consider the game of life to be pleasant, don't be so hard on yourself. My mother used to say never talk yourself down as your friends can do a much better job of it! If God accepts us as we are, why can't we do the same?

If we study the great men and women of the Bible, we will find that they did not compete with anyone else. As he was approaching death, Paul said: *I have fought a good fight, I have finished my course,*

I have kept the faith. 2Timothy 4:7

    The only course that Paul was concerned with was his course! He was not competing with another person; he was concerned only with his own walk in life which was to lead others to salvation. If we can leave competition aside, we can then be satisfied with ourselves as we walk in the path that the Lord has established for us. Paul also said: *For I say, through the grace given to me, to every one who is among you, not to think of himself more highly than he ought to think. But set your mind to be right-minded, even as God has dealt to every man the measure of faith.* Romans 12:3

    He said for us not to think *more* highly than we ought to think. So he said that we should think highly of ourselves, that we should have self confidence as God has given us that measure of faith. If God does not think down on us, why should we? If we would realize that God loves us, we will never have low self-esteem or be able to think down on ourselves again.

    Let's pray right now, "Lord, please let me see myself as You see me. Thank You."

Hmm, So You Have A Problem Workbook

Questions:

1. Who created us to be like Himself? _____
2. If so, we should not be _____ of His creation, even ourselves.
3. *When my bones were being formed, carefully put together in my mother's* _____ *...you saw me before I was born.*
4. *The days allotted to me had all been created in your* _____.
5. Our original bodies were determined while we were in our mother's _____.
6. What did Jesus tell the scribes was the foremost commandment? _____
7. Is it conceit to love ourselves and think well of ourselves if we love God first? _____
8. We are _____ in the eyes of God.
9. Many people who think down on themselves have established impossible _____ for themselves.
10. If God accepts us as we are, can we do the same? _____
11. If we study the great men and women of the bible, we find that they did not _____ with anyone else.
12. What course was Paul concerned with at the end of his life? _____
13. Paul said that _____ *has dealt to every man the* _____ *of faith.*

Discuss how we can overcome low self esteem and become the person the Lord created us to be.

Hmm, So You Have A Problem Workbook

Chapter 7

FEAR - FALSE EVENTS APPEAR TO BE REAL

Cowards die many times before their deaths; the valiant never taste of death but once. Julius Caesar II ii, Shakespeare

What an apt description of fear. False Events Appear to be Real. How many things we fear actually happen? Probably not most except the fear of dying. Death is inevitable - if we are prepared for it we will not fear it; if we continually fear it we will die daily in our thoughts.

The Psalmist said: *I will walk around freely because I sought out your guiding principles.* Psalm 119:45 The word freely means roomy in the Hebrew. Roomy - spacious - not confined into one small place. We can travel; meet new people, live life fully without fears if we seek out the guiding principles of God. What are they? We can know them and apply them by reading His Word the Bible.

It's a promise of God that we live freely without fear if we pursue the words and ways of God. John the apostle said: *There is no fear where love exists. Rather, perfect love banishes fear, for fear involves punishment, and the person who lives in fear has not been perfected in love.* 1John 4:18

Let's consider the example of a parent and a child. If the parent shows the child love, the child will be secure in that love, regardless of his environment. The child will respect the parent but respect is not fear of punishment. As we respect God and live in His word and promises, we do not live in fear of eternal damnation.

The Psalmist said: *The fear of the LORD is the beginning of wisdom. Good sense is shown by everyone who follows God's guiding principles. His praise continues forever.* Psalm 111:10

The word *fear* translated from the Hebrew means reverence and respect. Good understanding means intelligence, success, discretion, and wisdom. If we follow the commandments of God, He promises us good sense! Even the people who do not believe in God will probably attain success if they follow the precepts of God. Under communism in Russia, the State tried to abolish all religions and all things pertaining to religion, such as the Ten Commandments. The people were living such wild and uncontrollable lives that the state established rules for people to live by, which were almost the same as the Ten Commandments! Even in this country where some people are trying to abolish all references to the Ten Commandments, the people who are doing that will be hard pressed to live in a society where murder, adultery, disrespect of parents, lying, cheating, stealing, which are prohibited by the Ten Commandments, are all permitted.

We can conclude that the more love we have for God and the more love we let ourselves receive from God will conversely rid us of fear. If we truly believe that God created us and everything in the universe, how can we fear anything in our lives if we have given our lives to God? He Who can create out of nothing such a beautiful and harmonious world can surely watch over us. Jesus told us: *Aren't two sparrows sold for a penny? Not one of them will fall to the ground without your Father's permission. Every hair on your head has been counted. Don't be afraid! You are worth more than many sparrows.* Matthew 10:29-31

Can you comprehend someone who can count every hair on your head? God knows everything - the grand picture and the minutest details. Isn't He someone who can take all our fears away? If His eye is on the sparrow (as the hymn goes) then we know He watches us! What a wonderful promise!

So let's give ourselves over to the love of God and see how He banishes fear from our lives.

Hmm, So You Have A Problem Workbook

Questions:

1. Shakespeare said Cowards die many times before their deaths, the valiant never taste of death but _____.
2. _____ is inevitable - if we are prepared for it, we will not _____ it.
3. How can we know the guiding principles of God? _____
4. *There is no _____ where love exists.*
5. _____ is not fear of punishment.
6. The Psalmist said *the fear of God is the beginning of _____*.
7. The more love we have for God and the more love we let ourselves receive from God will conversely rid us of _____.
8. Jesus said _____ *be afraid! You are worth more than many sparrows.*

Discuss how when we give ourselves over to the love of God He banishes fear from our lives.

Chapter 8

DESPAIR - LET'S NOT GIVE INTO IT

I can do all things through Christ who strengthens me. Philippians 4:13

Despair - to lose hope, to be without hope, in the Greek, to be utterly at a loss.

A friend of mine, while in high school, entered a bicycle race. When he thought that he would not finish well, he stopped at a diner and had a huge breakfast. Can we say that he *despaired* of winning?

Do you remember the story of the little blue engine who kept saying as he was climbing a difficult hill, "I think I can, I think I can!" and he did it! So much depends upon our attitude. The apostle Paul probably had more troubles and discouragements than anyone else written of in the Bible, but he was able to say: *We are often troubled, but not crushed; sometimes in doubt, but never in despair.* 2Corinthians 4:8

Not crushed - not in despair. Crushed means to hem in closely, that is, to cramp. So Paul was surrounded by troubles, but did not give in to despair. Instead he said: *I can do all things through Christ who strengthens me.* Philippians 4:13

Paul was able to look beyond the circumstances. When we look at the circumstances, we can become overwhelmed. When we become overwhelmed, then we feel despair. Then the next thing that follows is giving up. If we have faith to believe that Jesus will strengthen us in any situation, then we can say as Paul said when he was approaching death: *I have done my best in the race, I have run the full distance, and I have kept the faith.* 2Timothy 4:7

Note that Paul did not say that he had won the race; he said that he had done his best. He does not compare himself to others. If we do not compare ourselves to others nor compete in life against others but walk in our own paths, then we will not despair or lose hope. God does not lose hope in us. He gives us many chances to come back to the life that He has planned for us. Why, then, should we become discouraged with ourselves and give up hope? As Paul said: *In view of all this, what can we say? If God is for us, who can be against us?* Romans 8:31

If the Creator of the universe is for us, how can we become discouraged? How can we lose hope when we know that He never gives up on us? Why shall we consider giving up when our magnificent and majestic and all powerful God does not despair of us? When we can come to the realization of seeing things in this way, we will never despair again! Let's say a prayer right now that we shall never despair again!

Hmm, So You Have A Problem Workbook

Questions:

1. *I can do all things through _____ who strengthens me.*
2. Despair means to lose _____, to be without _____ to be utterly at a loss.
3. So much depends on our _____.
4. The apostle Paul probably had more troubles and discouragements than anyone else but he was able to say *We are often troubled but not _____; sometimes in doubt, but never in _____*
5. He also said *I can do all things through _____ who strengthens me.*
6. When we look at the circumstances, we can become _____
7. Before Paul died, he looked back on his life and said *I have done my _____ in the race, I have run the full distance, and I have kept the _____.*
8. He did not say that he had _____ the race.
9. He does not _____ himself to others.
10. We should all walk in our own _____.
11. God does not lose _____ in us - He gives us many chances.

Discuss Paul's saying *In view of all this, what can we say? If God is for us, who can be against us?*

Hmm, So You Have A Problem Workbook

Chapter 9

CONTENTMENT, PEACE, AND HARMONY

I'm not saying this because I'm in any need. I've learned to be content in whatever situation I'm in. Philippians 4:11

Contentment is a state of mind in which our wishes and desires are in alignment with our circumstances in life, whatever they may be. It is the opposite of envy, avarice, ambition, greed, and anxiety.

We can reach a state of contentment when we have inner peace. How do we achieve inner peace? There is only one lasting way that I know, and that is to ask Jesus into our hearts and ask for forgiveness for all the sins that we have committed. When we commit our lives to the Lord, we can see beyond our limited circumstances to the Divine will of God in our lives. We can truly see that, as the apostle Paul said: *We know that God is always at work for the good of everyone who loves him. They are the ones God has chosen for his purpose.* Romans 8:28

Chosen for God's purpose! What a statement! Isn't life easy and happy when we allow God to be in control? What happened when we tried to take control? We screwed it up, didn't we??? When I was in control of my life, I used to run into roadblocks trying to solve my problems. Now I just go to the Lord and He opens the doors. We thought we were so wise and intelligent, but when we: *Trust GOD from the bottom of your heart; don't try to figure out everything on your own* Proverbs 3:5 , things start to work out for us.

When we trust God in our lives, He will give us the understanding that we need and life becomes easy and contented. We cannot enter into another person's mind, so why do we always try to figure out the motivations of another person? If we accept that God is in control of our lives, then we can accept that He also is in control of all lives. If others bother us, we know that He will handle the situations and we do not have to overreact.

The apostle Paul said: *Seeing it is a righteous thing with God to*

Hmm, So You Have A Problem Workbook

recompense tribulation to them that trouble you. 2Thessalonians 1:6

Wow! What do we have to worry about if we are in the will of God? Nothing! Why can't we spend our time here on earth in contentment? Let's consider the prophet Habbakuk. In the first chapter of Habbakuk he complained to the Lord about all that was happening around him and all the things over which he did not have control. Then in the second chapter, he climbed up to his high tower and set himself upon his watch and said he will watch and see what He (God) will say to him. *"And the Lord answered me."* Habbakuk 2:2 Isn't that the way our prayer life should be? We can come to the Lord with our problems and cares and unburden our souls to Him. But then, as Habbakuk did, we can set ourselves above our problems and watch and wait until we hear from the Lord for the solutions.

Habbakuk was able to say: *Even though the fig trees have no fruit and no grapes grow on the vines, even though the olive crop fails and the fields produce no grain, even though the sheep all die and the cattle stalls are empty, I will still be joyful and glad, because the LORD God is my savior. The Sovereign LORD gives me strength. He makes me sure-footed as a deer and keeps me safe on the mountains.* Habbakuk 3:17-19

He said he will be joyful and glad! Isn't that contentment?

What robs us of contentment? Could it be anxiety, fear, trying to control another person, anger, jealousy, envy - all the negative emotions? If we could examine ourselves as the apostle Paul told us to: *For if we would judge ourselves, we would not be judged* 1Corinthians 11:31 we can become content. *Judge* in the Greek means to separate thoroughly, discern. If we can judge the emotions in ourselves, determine if they are positive or if they are negative and thus determine our state of mind, then we can either thank God for contentment in our lives or ask God to remove the negative emotions from our lives so that we can become content. The apostle Paul was able to say: *I'm not saying this because I'm in any need. I've learned to be content in whatever situation I'm in.* Philippians 4:11. How did he learn to be content in whatever situation? Let's look at the preceding verses: *Finally, brothers, whatever is true, whatever is honorable,*

Hmm, So You Have A Problem Workbook

whatever is fair, whatever is pure, whatever is acceptable, whatever is commendable, if there is anything of excellence and if there is anything praiseworthy-keep thinking about these things. Likewise, keep practicing these things: what you have learned, received, heard, and seen in me. Then the God of peace will be with you. Philippians 4:8-9

Paul said to think about honorable, fair, pure, acceptable, commendable things. Then we can have the peace of the Lord. Consider - can you get angry or be upset while thinking about pleasant things? No! So why dwell on the unpleasant? If your past was unpleasant, examine it once, confess your sins, forgive the sins committed against you, and then forget it! Don't keep going back unless you wish to be miserable and discontented with life. You've heard the expression - today is the first day of the rest of your life. So for our first day, let us determine to be positive, to be thankful, and to be content!

Have you noticed something? Contented people do not complain. They accept situations knowing that God is in control and He will turn things around for their good. So when a situation seems bad, sit on your high tower as Habbakuk did and wait for an answer from the Lord. Life is so easy when we trust the Lord. Life is so hard when we try to do everything ourselves. So let's give that heavy burden to the Lord, rest in Him, and be content.

Hmm, So You Have A Problem Workbook

Questions:

1. Who had learned to be content in any situation he was in? _____
2. Contentment is a state of mind in which our _____ and our _____ are in alignment with our circumstances in life, whatever they may be.
3. It is the opposite of _____ _____ _____
4. If we have _____ _____ we can reach a state of contentment.
5. There are two ways to achieve inner peace _____ _____
6. We know that *God is always at work for the* _____ *of everyone who loves Him.*
7. *They are the ones God has chosen for His* _____.
8. If we allow God to be in control of our lives, we will be _____
9. When we trust God in our lives, He will give us the _____ we need.
10. We can come to the Lord with our problems and cares and then, as Habbakuk did, we can sit back until He gives us the _____.
11. The negative emotions, fear, anxiety, control, anger, envy, jealousy will rob us of _____
12. _____ means to separate thoroughly, discern.
13. If we judge ourselves we will not be _____.
14. What should we try to keep ourselves thinking about? _____
15. If our past was unpleasant, examine it _____, confess our sins, _____ others and then forget it!

Discuss the burdens we have given to the Lord and how He handled them through us.

35

Hmm, So You Have A Problem Workbook

Chapter 10

BETRAYAL - THE UNEXPECTED

Then Judas Iscariot, one of the twelve, went away to the chief priests so that he could betray Him to them. Mark 14:10

Have you ever been betrayed by a loved one, a person in whom you placed all your trust? In the First Testament the word betray means hurl, shoot, delude, betray as if causing to fall, beguile, deceive. In the New Testament, the word betray is always used in reference to the betrayal of Jesus. It means to surrender, yield up, deliver up, give up, put in prison. What a sad word and sad time when a loved one betrays us. It happened in a major way to Jesus, so are we surprised if it happens to us?

Remember the lady with the alabaster jar of precious ointment who anointed Jesus as He was at the house of Simon the leper in Mark chapter 14? *She broke the jar - she gave all she had - and poured it on Him. Some of the apostles* (we believe especially Judas) *were incensed because the ointment was very expensive. Jesus reprimanded them: Some who were there said to one another in irritation, "Why was the perfume wasted like this? This perfume could have been sold for more than 300 denarii and the money given to the destitute." So they got extremely angry with her. But Jesus said, "Leave her alone. Why are you bothering her? She has done a beautiful thing for me."* Mark 14:4-6

Almost immediately after this, Judas went to the chief priests and betrayed Jesus to them.

An interesting thing about Judas' betrayal is that all the versions of the Bible that I have, use a conjunction - either and or then - to describe when Judas went to the chief priests following the reprimand that Jesus gave him for being greedy. He had been told the truth about his greedy conduct and so resented Jesus telling him the truth that he betrayed him. The thirty pieces of silver were mentioned after his betrayal. The other apostles received the reprimand. Judas did not receive it, not having a teachable spirit.

Jesus was not political. He spoke and did what was true, not what was politically correct. One of the saddest verses in the Bible is: *For He knew that because of envy they had handed Him over.* Matthew 27:18 They (the religious leaders) envied Him because He was expounding on the truth, the truth that because of their religious system, they were unable or unwilling to see. These men were comfortable in their religion, being respected by the people as leaders, when they were in truth the blind leading the blind. They were unwilling to look at themselves clearly, see their sins, and beg God for forgiveness. So they betrayed Him! What a sad commentary on human life. Let us never believe that without the grace of God, we can make it.

Let's pray right now to maintain a teachable spirit so that we can be corrected by the Lord.

Hmm, So You Have A Problem Workbook

Questions:

1. If we are betrayed, should we be surprised as our _____ was also betrayed.
2. What was the ultimate betrayal of Judas? _____
3. When Jesus reprimanded the apostles, who did not receive it? _____
4. The reason he did not receive correction was because he did not have a _____ spirit.
5. Was Jesus political? _____ Did He always speak the truth? _____
6. Why did the religious leaders hand Him over? _____
7. What kind of a spirit should we maintain? _____
8. Can we really make it without the grace of God? _____

Discuss times when we were betrayed and how we reacted to it and how we would react today.

Chapter 11

HOW CAN WE HANDLE REJECTION?

He was despised, and rejected of men; a man of sorrows, and acquainted with grief: and as one from whom men hide their face he was despised; and we esteemed him not. Isaiah 53:3

We are programmed to accept all kinds of human behavior. However, the one behavior we are not programmed to accept is rejection. Studies have shown that when babies are rejected and not held for long periods of time, they have a terribly hard time bonding to anyone.

The person who initiates a divorce usually adjusts very easily to their new life - but the rejected person usually has a very hard time adjusting. (One does not choose to be rejected - it is thrust upon him.)

If someone hates us, we can adjust to that hate. If someone is jealous or envious of us, we can adjust to that jealousy or envy. However if someone rejects us, we do not have any emotion in us to adjust.

Consider the passage where Isaiah prophesied about Jesus: *He was despised, and rejected of men; a man of sorrows, and acquainted with grief: and as one from whom men hide their face he was despised; and we esteemed him not.* Isaiah 53:3 To not esteem in the Hebrew (Isaiah was written in Hebrew) means to make no account of, not to consider, not to regard. Isn't that a good description of rejection? When it happens, we feel a void - we no longer have a place in the other's life, and as we feel displaced, we realize we are being treated as if we do not exist. The emotional pain is unbearable. The person does not want us around, nor does he consider or have regard for us. The word forsaken in the Hebrew means rejected, vacant, destitute. Vacant - empty. That place that we once had in a person's life is now empty - that person does not now want us in his life.

There is a solution to the heartache of rejection and that solution is Jesus! Jesus took all our rejection on His way to the cross. Peter denied Him three times and all the apostles who walked with Jesus for three years and saw His love and goodness and all the wonderful miracles He performed fled when He was arrested in the Garden. ... *then all the disciples deserted him and ran away.* Matthew 26:56

Jesus prophesied: *"Behold, an hour is coming, and has already come, for you to be scattered, each to his own home, and to leave Me alone; and yet I am not alone, because the Father is with Me."* John 16:32

Jesus said, *yet I am not alone*! The only way that Jesus the Man endured such rejection is because the Father was with Him! The only way that we can deal with it is if God is with us! We can take all those hurts to the Cross of Jesus and lay them at His feet and know that the Father is with us! Only Jesus makes a way for our healing and that way is the way of the Cross. If we do not get healed by Jesus from the power of rejection, we will always feel that hurt and emptiness in our innermost being. So many people have so many problems all throughout their lives. They may go through therapy for years when they can just go to the Cross of Jesus, as He appealed to us to go to Him for help: *"Come to Me, all who are weary and heavy-laden, and I will give you rest. Take My yoke upon you and learn from Me, for I am gentle and humble in heart, and you will find rest for your souls. For My yoke is easy and My burden is light."* Matthew 11:28-30

Yoke means coupling, the beam of a balance. A yoke is used to harness two oxen together so that they can work together. Jesus is asking us to couple with Him! To feel His love and the joy that heals us from all hurts, especially rejection. Jesus said He will give us rest. Rest from anxiety, fear, heartbreak, and most of all, from rejection! When He said rest for our souls, the word means recreation, intermission. He will recreate our souls! He will make them new again and heal the pain that rejection causes. The healing cannot be given from one person to another; it is supernatural and can only come from God through Jesus. Time will dull our pain, but if we are not able to completely give it over to Jesus, it will always be deep inside us. So, why not now, turn to Jesus and give it all to Him.

Hmm, So You Have A Problem Workbook

Questions:

1. The one behavior we are not programmed to accept is _____.
2. One does not _____ to be rejected - it is thrust on them.
3. Is there any emotion with which we can combat rejection? _____
4. Isaiah said about _____ - *he was despised and rejected of man.*
5. If we are rejected, do we have a place in that person's life? _____
6. What or who is the solution to rejection? _____
7. Was He ever rejected? _____ Especially on His way to the cross? _____
8. Was the Father with Him? _____
9. Does He offer to carry our burdens with Him? _____
10. Who can heal the pain of rejection? _____
11. Is it supernatural? _____

Discuss how you have handled rejection in the past and how you will handle it if it occurs in the future.

Chapter 12

FAMILIARITY BREEDS CONTEMPT

And so they rejected him. Jesus said to them, "A prophet is respected everywhere except in his hometown and by his own family." Matthew 13:57

Why is it that a person can be so respected by others, while being rejected by his own people and family?

Years ago, when my father died, I took some of the beautiful stones he had collected to make into rings for my daughter, step daughter, and daughters in law. I said to the silversmith, "Your family must be so happy with the works that you do", but she replied, "No, they are sick of them." She did beautiful work, but her family held her in low esteem.

Why are family members so loath to give encouragement to friends and other family members? Why do husbands and wives talk each other down? The one place we expect to be accepted is in our own family. Why did Jesus' hometown people and family reject Him? *They said: "Isn't he the carpenter's son? Isn't Mary his mother, and aren't James, Joseph, Simon, and Judas his brothers? Aren't all his sisters living here? Where did he get all this?"* Matthew 13: 55-56

Why didn't they listen to all this? Perhaps Solomon gave us an answer: *Again, I considered all travail, and every right work, that for this a man is envied of his neighbor. This is also vanity and vexation of spirit.* Ecclesiastes 4:4

For every right or successful work, a man is often envied by his neighbor. So it's really jealousy that triggers the contempt. Instead of encouraging a loved one's endeavors, many people envy his or her success. What a world this might be if we encouraged each other rather than talked each other down! Let's not envy family or friends; rather let's be happy for their success. Let's not compete with one another; instead let's work together to accomplish more.

Shall we pray right now that the Lord will open the eyes of our hearts to encourage family members and friends and to eradicate all traces of envy.

Hmm, So You Have A Problem Workbook

Questions:

1. The one place we expect to be accepted is in our own _____.
2. What did they call Jesus? _____
3. Solomon said *that for this a man is* _____ *by his neighbor*.
4. It may be _____ that triggers unacceptance.
5. Also it may be _____

Discuss how we can work together on a common goal to accomplish much.

Chapter 13

FORGIVENESS - A DIFFICULT VIRTUE

But if you do not forgive, your Father in heaven will not forgive your sins. Mark 11:26

But I can't forgive him! You are right! It is often impossible to forgive someone. The mean actions, the horrible words, the breaking of trust - all of those offenses can cause us to hate the person, never forgive or forget the injuries. So why did Jesus tell us to forgive our enemies? Thirty times forgive, forgives, or forgiving is written in the New Testament and 28 times forgiven is written. Forgive means to send, to let go. The same Greek word for *forgive* is translated *remit* in John chapter 20. John writes about the appearance of Jesus to the apostles after His death and resurrection.

Then it being evening on that day, the first of the Sabbaths, and the doors having been locked where the disciples were assembled because of fear of the Jews, Jesus came and stood in the midst and said to them, Peace to you. And saying this, He showed them His hands and side. Then seeing the Lord, the disciples rejoiced. Then Jesus said to them again, Peace to you. As the Father has sent Me, I also send you. And saying this, He breathed on them and said to them, Receive the Holy Spirit. Of whomever you may remit the sins, they are remitted to them. Of whomever you hold, they have been held. John 20:19-23

The forgiveness, as it appears, is up to us. We can make the decision to forgive. Let's examine verse 23. If we remit people's sins, they are sent away or forgiven. When we get a bill in the mail, it usually says, "Send your payment with your remittance." Once we have sent the check or money order, it is remitted unto the other party. We never see that bill again. Then Jesus said if we keep or retain people's sins, or hold onto them, then we are the ones who have to continually deal with them. Once we have remitted the offenses, sent them away, payment full, we no longer have to deal with the hurts.

Hmm, So You Have A Problem Workbook

The other people have to deal with their sins now.

If we retain their sins or offenses, then we continually deal with them. Over and over the despicable things that people have done to us are reviewed in our minds and hearts and we become miserable human beings, people who have few friends (unless we are drinking and feeding on other people who are miserable). But if we send away the offenses, then we are free, and the people who dealt the blows have to deal with their actions. Do you see how easy it is, with Jesus' teachings, to let go and forgive offenses? No wonder Jesus said: *Therefore, if the Son sets you free, you are free indeed.* John 8:36

Just before Jesus died on the cross, He said, *"It is finished."* John 19:30 The word *finished* comes from a Greek word which means stamped on receipts, paid in full. Isn't that like the word remit? So it seems that since He paid the price for the remittance of our sins, we also have to remit the sins of others against us.

Do we trust the person again? The word trust means to have faith in a person or thing, to credit. Trust is earned by actions so it takes time to trust a person again. Can we love them and bless them? Jesus said we can: *but I say to you, Love your enemies; bless those cursing you, do well to those hating you; and pray for those abusing and persecuting you...* Matthew 5:44

Bless means to speak well of, to wish to prosper. Prosper means to succeed in their lives. Jesus said we can, so we can wish well to the person who is cursing us. If we say in our hearts or to the person, "Go to hell", we are not wishing well to the person. If we are rejoicing when the person falls, then we still have anger and unforgiveness in our hearts. We still are retaining the sins of another! When we can pray for that person who did us wrong, then we know we are on our way to recovery from the injuries of another.

One litmus test of forgiveness is that we no longer even think about the offenses of another. Jesus said at the cross: *And when they came on the place being called Skull, they crucified Him and the criminals there, one on the right, and one on the left. And Jesus said, Father, forgive them, for they do not know what they are doing.* Luke 23:33-34

They don't know what they are doing! So let us wish the persons well, hope they realize some day what they have done, and send those offenses away so that we can go on with our lives and fully recover from the hurts and offenses of other people. Is there any among us that has not offended? And if we ask forgiveness from God, has He forgiven us? He promised us: *As far as the east is from the west, so far has He removed our transgressions from us.* Psalm 103:12

Let's consider the east from the west. When David wrote this psalm, where he was living, if you went east you would get to modern day Iraq or Iran and then turn back and head west to the Mediterranean as the people had not yet discovered China or America. So David was thus speaking prophetically in the psalm. Now we know if we go east we will never go west. However, if we go north we will eventually go south! So David, not knowing geographically what he was writing wrote what the Lord put in his heart prophetically about the abundant forgiveness of God.

So let's pray to remit or send away all the hurts and negative thinking about the past and go on to a free life in Jesus!

Hmm, So You Have A Problem Workbook

Questions:

1. Sometimes it seems _____ to forgive someone.
2. Forgive means to _____, to let _____.
3. After the resurrection, when Jesus appeared to his disciples, after he breathed on them and said *Receive ye the Holy Spirit,* he also *said what sins you _____ are remitted unto them, what sins you _____ are _____*.
4. Who suffers when we do not forgive? _____
5. If we retain peoples sins against us, who continually has to deal with them? _____
6. If we send away the sins, who becomes free? _____
7. What did it mean when Jesus said *it is finished*? _____
8. If Jesus told us to love our enemies, is it possible? _____
9. If we forget about the offenses, we can know we are well on our way to _____.

Discuss how with the help of Jesus, we have been able to forgive.

Chapter 14

HOW TO REGAIN TRUST

Trust in the Lord with all your heart and do not lean on your own understanding. Proverbs 3:5

The word *trust* in the Hebrew means to hie (run) for refuge, be confident or sure, be bold, hope. Solomon, perhaps the wisest man who had ever lived until the time of Jesus, advised us to trust in the Lord and not lean on our own understanding! When he was to become king to succeed his father David to the throne, God asked him what he wanted and he replied wisdom. God gave him wisdom but also prosperity to reward him for asking for wisdom.

If we study Psalm 116, we will find that the Psalmist said in verse 11 *all men are liars*. He was disappointed in mankind before he learned to trust in the Lord. Trust can be broken in many ways, one of which is adultery. In Psalm 116, the Psalmist said: *...I found trouble and sorrow*. Psalm 116:3 The word trouble in the Hebrew means tightness, transitively a female rival! Could the author be a female? What can be worse to a woman than a female rival!! We have control over ourselves, but usually we cannot control another person, especially when that person is tempted by *...the strange woman, From the adulteress who flatters with her words.* Proverbs 2:16

It is interesting to note that the strange woman, the adulteress, is not described as beautiful, charming, and intelligent; she is described as someone who flatters with her words. The man is seduced by flattery! She knows exactly what to say to make the man feel wanted and attractive. This explains why some men leave their wives for someone who is not as nice or attractive or interesting. The man has been beguiled by smooth talk. This is why the Lord cautions us throughout the Bible to beware of flattery.

When I was teaching the women in the jail and told them the meaning of the word trouble in Psalm 116 was a female rival - I was surprised to see their frustration. Those poor women have no means of keeping their loved ones. Unfortunately, many of their loved ones were the ones who got them into trouble in the first place!

When a person has broken the trust in a marriage, forgiveness can come through prayer and understanding but trust takes longer to return. I caution the women that their families might need time to trust them again. However, when their families would see that the women were really trying to abstain from drugs or other things that brought them to jail, they should eventually trust them again.

There is one person in the world whom we can trust explicitly and that Person is God. He promised us in Hebrews: *...for God has said, "I will never leave you or abandon you."* Hebrews 13:5

Let's pray now that if trust is a problem in a relationship we will regain trust in our loved ones and they will in us.

Hmm, So You Have A Problem Workbook

Questions:

1. The word trust means to _____ for refuge.
2. Who advised us to trust in the Lord and lean not on our own understanding? _____
3. Trouble means tightness, transitively a _____ rival.
4. We can have control over ourselves but not _____
5. The strange woman is not described as beautiful but as one who _____ with her mouth.
6. When trust in a marriage is broken, can it ever be restored? _____
7. Who is the one person in the world that said *I will never leave you or abandon you?* _____

Discuss how we have lost trust in a person and have regained it by prayer.

Chapter 15

LACK OF COMMITMENT

Elijah challenged the people: "How long are you going to sit on the fence? If GOD is the real God, follow him; if it's Baal, follow him. Make up your minds!" Nobody said a word; nobody made a move. 1Kings 18:21

Someone might say, "One day I want to marry him, the next day I don't want to. One day I want to change jobs, the next day I guess I'll stay where I am. One day I feel like reading my Bible and going to church, the next day I feel like just vegging out. One day I think euthanasia and abortion are wrong, the next day I think that maybe they are OK." Have you ever had similar thoughts?

The people at the time of Elijah were suffering from spiritual drought, which leads to lack of commitment. Notice from the Scripture that Elijah was challenging the people to make a decision for God. Nobody said a word; nobody made a move. The King James Version calls it *"halt ye between two opinions."* Halt means to hop, skip over, hesitate, limp, or dance. What an apt description of someone who hops back and forth between two opinions.

James said: *Don't think you're going to get anything from the Master that way, adrift at sea, keeping all your options open.* James 1:7-8 Keeping all your options open! Skipping or hopping from one opinion to another, never making a commitment or decision!

I was saved by grace during the spiritual revival that rocked New England, the frozen chosen, during the '70's. I was working in a shoe factory as the only programmer. The comptroller of the company was saved first, then I was saved, then the office manager, the human resources manager, and so on throughout the whole factory - floor ladies, foremen, and workers. We used to sing heartily, "I have decided to follow Jesus, no turning back, no turning back!" It was a wonderful company to work for! One floor lady was so filled with the Lord that she used to hug the women when they didn't feel well and pray silently over them. I later saw her about eight years after I left the company. I asked her how she was doing and at that time she was really lukewarm for the Lord. I couldn't believe it! She had stayed in a spiritually dry church, didn't read her Bible or pray as she used to. What a sad story. The comptroller went on to be an elder of his church; I conducted prison ministry and started Bible studies at home and at work. Almost everyone else had also stayed on fire for the Lord. Truly, spiritual drought leads to lack of commitment.

Jesus was very explicit about lack of commitment: *'I know your deeds, that you are neither cold nor hot; I wish that you were cold or hot. So because you are lukewarm, and neither hot nor cold, I will spit you out of My mouth. Because you say, "I am rich, and have become wealthy, and have need of nothing," and you do not know that you are wretched and miserable and poor and blind and naked...* Revelation 3:15-17

Wow! That is powerful! When we think we have it made without the Lord, He calls us wretched, miserable, poor, blind, and naked. He also said: *I advise you to buy from Me gold refined by fire so that you may become rich, and white garments so that you may clothe yourself, and that the shame of your nakedness will not be revealed; and eye salve to anoint your eyes so that you may see. Those whom I love, I reprove and discipline; therefore be zealous and repent. Behold, I stand at the door and knock; if anyone hears My voice and opens the door, I will come in to him and will dine with him, and he with Me.* Revelation 3:18-20 The Lord is calling us to commitment today. Let's not wait until judgment day. Let's make a commitment to the Lord today, right now, and He will also help us make any other commitments we need to make.

Hmm, So You Have A Problem Workbook

Questions:

1. The people at the time of Elijah were suffering from _____ drought.
2. Someone who _____ between two opinions means to hop, skip, vacillate.
3. James said *keeping all your options open will not get you anything from the* _____.
4. If you don't read your bible and stay in a spiritually dry church you may lose your _____ for the Lord.
5. Those who are neither hot nor cold are warned by Jesus in Revelation that *He will* _____ *them out of his mouth*.
6. He calls people like that to be _____ and repent.
7. The Lord is calling us to _____ at this time.

Discuss any times you felt like giving up and were indifferent to the Lord and how you repented and changed.

Chapter 16

DON'T DELAY - JUST DO IT!

...don't get worked up about what may or may not happen tomorrow. Matthew 6:34

A person might wishfully say, "I'm going to get myself out of debt. I'm going to write a book. I'm going to get my GED. I'm going to get a job. I'm going to get my own apartment."

This person looks at the whole picture and it overwhelms him. Then he ends up doing nothing. The whole is the sum of the parts. If you attempt a project in life, just go at it one step at a time to accomplish it.

I was a system analyst/programmer starting a new job at a firm. When I went there, I encountered pages of projects which were to be completed. So I had a meeting with my boss and prioritized the projects. I went to work on each one, one at a time. After a period of time, the projects were finished! Of course, almost immediately, there were new projects. However, had I looked at the list initially as a whole I would have been discouraged and probably walked out the door, never completing any. By attacking the list, project by project, I was able to finish it.

So it is in life. If we look at the grand scheme of things, we may get discouraged and not accomplish anything. Success is accomplishing today what is for today. Jesus said: *Give your entire attention to what God is doing right now, and don't get worked up about what may or may not happen tomorrow. God will help you deal with whatever hard things come up when the time comes.* Matthew 6:34

How many people plan on retirement all their lives and just live for the day when they will retire. When the day finally comes, they either get sick or die or become infirm or just plain bored. Now is the time to enjoy life, to do the things you wish to do, or to at least attempt to.

Hmm, So You Have A Problem Workbook

A few years ago my husband and I were on vacation in Florida. We saw a section of condos on the beach which we felt was ideal for us. So we put a deposit on one and went back to our hotel. When we told some friends about it, the husband looked so forlorn. They were about 10 years older than we were and his wife was in a wheelchair. He said, sadly, "You have to do it when you want to do it."

As it happened, we went back to New England, sold our house, gave our notices at work, and moved to sunny Florida. It seemed like the right time to just do it and we did! So instead of having regrets, we are enjoying our lives. When we made that decision to just do it, we were in our sixties and approaching retirement. I don't advocate everyone quitting their jobs and becoming beach bums, but if you wish a positive change of any kind in your lives, then have the courage to just do it!

Let's pray right now for wisdom and courage to accomplish that which we should do in our lives.

Hmm, So You Have A Problem Workbook

Questions:

1. If we look at the whole picture, we can become _____
2. If the whole is the sum of the parts, in order to accomplish it we should take _____ step at a time.
3. _____ is accomplishing today what is for today.
4. _____ said *give your entire attention to what God is doing right now.*
5. *And don't get* _____ *up about what may or may not happen tomorrow.*

Discuss good decisions you have made to accomplish for today what is for today.

Chapter 17

INSPIRATION - WHERE DOES IT COME FROM?

...but with God all things are possible. Matthew 19:26

Who or what inspires us? The word *inspire* is from the old French or Latin. It means to breathe in; to draw into the lungs or inhale; to influence, stimulate, or impel, as to some creative or effective effort; to guide or motivate by divine influence; to arouse a thought or feeling; to cause to be written or said. What or who influences us? How do some people by inspiration invent, discover, write, or compose? What brings it about? The answer seems to be that it comes either from another person or an idea that is born within us.

Shall we consider another person or persons inspiring us? During the time of the great classical composers - one after another wrote music that is even now everlasting, beautiful, and inspirational. Do you agree that the excellence of one composer inspired the other composers to create music that is harmonious, melodious, soothing, and peaceful? During the same period, many classic books were written and beautiful and lasting art and architecture was created. Was it a time of great inspiration or did one person inspire another person to greatness? It seems that we might agree that it must have started with one person. After that, either the other people were inspired within themselves or were inspired by the preceding persons.

So let's examine how the greatness could come about in the first creative person and in so doing learn if we can also have that inspiration. Jesus said: *...but with God all things are possible.* Matthew 19:26 Possible infers powerful, capable, able.

The apostle James said: *Every good gift and every perfect present comes from heaven; it comes down from God.* James 1:17 Inspiration is a good gift, so it must come from Heaven, from God. If with God "*all things are possible*", then inspiration surely comes from our relationship with God.

Elihu, the youngest and wisest of Job's advisors said to Job:

Hmm, So You Have A Problem Workbook

Although God speaks again and again, no one pays attention to what he says. At night when people are asleep, God speaks in dreams and visions. Job 33:14-15

    Have you ever heard people say, "I will sleep on that decision"? Or have you ever woken up inspired? We can be unaware that God is helping us in our dreams to make the right decisions! So also will God inspire us to do great things, if we rest in Him and allow Him to speak to our spirits. Living with God is very easy if we do what the Psalmist advised us: *Be still, and know that I am God...* Psalm 46:10 Be still means to fall, let go, be faint. When we surrender our wills to God and let Him be in control of our lives, He will inspire us to do the works that He has planned for us to accomplish since the foundation of the earth.

    Some Christians say that being a Christian is hard. I find that life is so much easier than when I was not saved. As a Christian, if I can fall, let go, and let God take control of my life, it follows an easier pattern. When He is in control, I can be in spirit or inspired by Him and by being obedient to His will, I can accomplish that which He has inspired me to do. When the task is accomplished, I can rest in the words of Zephaniah the prophet: *The LORD your God is with you; his power gives you victory. The LORD will take delight in you, and in his love he will give you new life. He will sing and be joyful over you.* Zephaniah 3:17 *The Lord our God will sing over us!* Praise God!

    Let's pray that we will fulfill all that the Lord has inspired us to do.

Hmm, So You Have A Problem Workbook

Questions:

1. *With _____ all things are possible.*
2. _____ is to stimulate, influence, to arouse a thought or a feeling.
3. Can other people inspire us? _____
4. Possible infers _____ _____ _____
5. Where does every good gift come from? _____
6. Inspiration is a good gift. So it must come from _____ originally.
7. Does God speak to us in dreams sometimes? _____
8. When we _____ our lives to Him, will He inspire us?
9. Does the Lord sing over us? _____

Discuss times when you were inspired to do something that the Lord had put on your heart.

Chapter 18

IMPULSIVE BEHAVIOR GETS US IN TROUBLE

Then a scribe came and said to Him, Teacher, I will follow You wherever You go. Matthew 8:19

When Jesus explained to the scribe that the foxes have holes and the birds of the air have nests but He did not have anywhere to live, we do not hear about that scribe again. Impulsively the scribe wanted to follow Jesus, but he had not considered the cost.

One of the women in my jail ministry was so happy because another woman who came in prophesied that she was to become a minister, so my friend thought she would not have to work! Little did she realize that being a minister can be harder work than any other profession. Many ministers have outside jobs in addition to pastoral duties and often counsel, have administrative duties, etc. A Greek word for minister used by Luke once and by Paul once means under oarsman or galley slave. All other times the word means deacon. Let's consider a galley slave. He works to bring people from one place to another and when he dies, he is thrown overboard. Isn't that the way a true minister should be? We should transport people into a higher place and when God is finished with us, we die and another takes our place! Impulsive behavior is not considering the cost, not thinking it through.

One day, I was riding along a beach road, and I saw a man dressed in prison orange cutting through the walkway to the beach. Strange, I thought, until I crossed the causeway and saw a gang of men dressed in orange doing road work. The prisoner may have had weeks to go before release but just had to obey his impulse to flee. He probably received 6 to 12 more months for trying to escape! Another example of impulsive behavior!

"I want it now, so I'll do it now!" is impulsive behavior regardless of the consequences. People sometimes say that an affair just happened. However, if actions leading to an affair are examined, there are definite steps that take place to have that affair. One has to arrange to meet the person, find a rendezvous place, and lie to his spouse before the affair is consummated. So nothing just happens.

God gave us a brain so we could think things over before we make decisions. Of course, we can over analyze and then do nothing. However, it is wisdom to weigh the consequences before we act. Impulsive behavior usually results in regrets. If we can think about the results, consider the cost, and then make decisions, we may have very little to regret.

Let's ask the Lord to give us wisdom so that we will not act impulsively.

Hmm, So You Have A Problem Workbook

Questions:

1. What behavior did the scribe display when saying he would follow Jesus? _____
2. What did the Greek word for minister used by Luke mean? _____
3. Impulsive behavior is not considering the _____, not thinking it _____
4. Does an affair just happen? _____
5. God gave us a _____ so that we can _____ before acting.

Discuss times when an impulsive decision got you into trouble.

Hmm, So You Have A Problem Workbook

Chapter 19

WISDOM OF SOLOMON

But as for you, Daniel, conceal these words and seal up the book until the end of time, many will go back and forth, and knowledge will increase. Daniel 12:4

Wisdom is knowledge applied. We can have all the knowledge in the world, but if it is not applied in our lives, what good is it? Knowledge is said to be increasing exponentially now with PCs and the internet. But are people living wiser lives? From the news reports, it doesn't seem so.

Daniel's name means judge. The word judge means to litigate, avenge, contend, defend, plead, reason, rule. Long before the birth of Christ, Moses had established judges to help him rule. After Moses and Joshua died, God would periodically designate judges such as Deborah, Samson, and Gideon, to rule all the people. At that time, there were only scrolls of the Word of God which were studied by the rabbinical students and priests. They were not available to the common people, so God gave them judges with wisdom to rule. Unlike other prophets or judges who preached the word of God to the unhearing people, Deborah would sit under her palm tree between Ramah and Bethel, and the people would come to her for judgments and wisdom.

At that time the king of Hazor ruled the people harshly. It was Deborah who caused the people to rise up against him. Under her supervision preparations for battle were made to overthrow the oppressor. Barak was called to take command of the army. But he was unwilling to go without Deborah so she went with him and led the attack.

Because he was unwilling to go without her, she told him that he would not receive honor and that the Lord would deliver Sisera, the leader of the opposition, into the hands of a woman. Deborah didn't say how or why this would be, she just knew in her heart that the victory would be gained by a woman. Oftentimes this is how the prophetic is with God. He does not give specifics; he just touches the hearts of His people with knowledge of future events. After the attack by Deborah's army, the army of Sisera was almost wholly routed. When Sisera fled from the battle, he went to the tent of Jael, the wife of Heber, and when he rested, Jael killed him. So the honor for the victory went to a woman, actually two women. Deborah showed great wisdom, even leading the people into battle, which was unheard of by a woman in those days. Deborah and Jael's wisdom came directly from God.

Another person in more recent history, who showed great wisdom was a Viennese doctor named Dr. Semmelweis who lived in the 1800s. At that time, women were dying during childbirth from Puerperal Fever. They would deliver their babies in the streets rather than go to hospitals, because so many were dying in those institutions. The physicians at that time would cut up cadavers, wipe their hands on their frock coats, and then go to the hospital to deliver babies.

Dr. Semmelweis set up basins in which doctors would wash their hands before delivery, and the death rate was greatly reduced. After a while, he noticed in his record keeping that the patients assigned to a particular doctor were dying. When he investigated, he found that the doctor was not washing his hands! The doctor was too proud to take Dr. Semmelweis' instructions! How much this is like knowledge not applied! Aren't we blessed today to have the Bible so available to us? The Bible contains so much wisdom and knowledge. If we apply what we learn from the Word of God, we will have wisdom. If we do not apply biblical knowledge, we will just have a lot of words in our head that avail us nothing. We probably will be like the doctor who refused to wash his hands if we refuse to wash ourselves in the Word.

So let's pray right now to receive grace from God to apply the knowledge that we are learning from the Word to our lives and ultimately to have increased wisdom.

Hmm, So You Have A Problem Workbook

Questions:

1. _____ is knowledge applied.
2. Daniel's name means _____.
3. The word _____ means to litigate, avenge, contend, defend, reason, rule.
4. Moses established _____ to help him rule.
5. There were no written materials for the people, only scrolls for the scribes and priests so God gave good _____ to rule.
6. _____ was a prophetess who gave good counsel for battle from oppression.
7. If we apply what we learn from the bible, we will have _____.

Discuss how you applied biblical wisdom in your own life.

Hmm, So You Have A Problem Workbook

Chapter 20

PRIDE - THE INSIDIOUS EMOTION

Pride goes before destruction... Proverbs 16:18

The world regards pride as an attribute; God regards pride as a stumbling block or a detriment. How many parents and teachers tell their children how proud they are of them? We have pride in workmanship, citizenship, being a good parent. The word pride in the Hebrew means arrogance, excellency, majesty, pomp, swelling, to strut, haughtiness (as evinced by the attitude). In the Greek the word means to inflate with self conceit, high-minded, to be lifted up with pride, haughtiness, appearing above others, conspicuous, haughty. Is it any wonder that the apostle Peter said: *Likewise, younger ones be subject to older ones; and all being subject to one another. Put on humility, because God sets Himself against proud ones, but He gives grace to humble ones.* 1Peter 5:5

The very proud person usually feels that he does not need God because he is a god unto himself. The humble person sees himself as he really is, and in deep need of God.

Jesus often told stories in the form of parables (short narratives to teach moral lessons). The parables were often directed to people who thought they were better than others and who looked down on everyone else: *"Two men went up into the temple to pray, one a Pharisee and the other a tax collector. The Pharisee stood and was praying this to himself: 'God, I thank You that I am not like other people: swindlers, unjust, adulterers, or even like this tax collector. I fast twice a week; I pay tithes of all that I get.' But the tax collector, standing some distance away, was even unwilling to lift up his eyes to heaven, but was beating his breast, saying, 'God, be merciful to me, the sinner!' I tell you, this man went to his house justified rather than the other; for everyone who exalts himself will be humbled, but he who humbles himself will be exalted."* Luke 18:10-14

Jesus explained the meaning of the parable from the beginning.

Hmm, So You Have A Problem Workbook

He was speaking to those who trusted in themselves rather than in God.

The Pharisees were the religious leaders of that day. The tax collectors were looked down upon because some collected more taxes than those asked for by Rome. They then kept the overage for themselves. They weren't all evil but had the reputation for being evil.

Consider that the Pharisee stood and was praying this to himself. Apparently he wasn't even praying to God! What pride he had. He was congratulating himself on not being a swindler, unjust, or an adulterer. He did not acknowledge that the fruit of temperance or self control comes from the Holy Spirit, not from us.

The prophet Isaiah said: *For all of us have become like one who is unclean, And all our righteous deeds are like a filthy garment; And all of us wither like a leaf, And our iniquities, like the wind, take us away.* Isaiah 64:6

If we can realize that it is by the grace of God that we stand, we may never become proud.

The Pharisee was bragging about going without food or fasting twice a week. Did you ever fast and think, "This is great - I will lose some weight"? I have. I can assure you that I got nowhere on that fast! Fasting, if done to come closer to the Lord and to bring the flesh under subjection, is worthwhile. However, if done for other reasons as the Pharisee had, it accomplishes nothing.

Jesus said: *Beware of practicing your righteousness before men to be noticed by them; otherwise you have no reward with your Father who is in heaven. So when you give to the poor, do not sound a trumpet before you, as the hypocrites do in the synagogues and in the streets, so that they may be honored by men. Truly I say to you, they have their reward in full. But when you give to the poor, do not let your left hand know what your right hand is doing, so that your giving will be in secret; and your Father who sees what is done in secret will reward you.* Matthew 6:1-4

The Pharisee was blowing his own horn or trumpet, as Jesus told us: *"But the tax collector, standing some distance away, was even unwilling to lift up his eyes to heaven, but was beating his breast, saying, 'God, be merciful to me, the sinner!'"* Luke 18:13

Hmm, So You Have A Problem Workbook

Be merciful to me, the sinner. He was not involved in what others were doing or had done, when he prayed to God, he was involved in himself alone. He called himself the sinner. He wasn't comparing himself to anyone. He knew that, on his own, he fell short of the glory of God. Our great apostle Paul said: *It is a trustworthy statement, deserving full acceptance, that Christ Jesus came into the world to save sinners, among whom I am foremost of all.* 1Timothy 1:15

Foremost means chief. Paul could say that he was chief among sinners. Paul never forgot from where he came. He realized that all the miracles that Jesus did through him and all the grace that the Holy Spirit poured out onto him were gifts from God. He did nothing but humbly accept everything that the Lord bestowed upon him.

How many times do we see parents who had unruly children themselves criticize other parents. They actually believe they were great parents! Some people like to rewrite history. However, the humble person realizes that all grace and all gifts come from God. We have an obligation to use the gifts of God for His glory not for ours. For example, gospel singers who go public after which all kinds of troubles enter their lives. Did they remove the protection of the Lord when they went into the secular world? The promise from God if we stay close to Him is: *God is keeping careful watch over us and the future.* 1Peter 1:5 Not all who leave the church for secular glory fall, but many do.

The book of Proverbs has much to say about pride: *When pride comes, then comes dishonor, But with the humble is wisdom.* Proverbs 11:2 *Pride goes before destruction, And a haughty spirit before stumbling. It is better to be humble in spirit with the lowly than to divide the spoil with the proud.* Proverbs 16:18-19 *Through insolence comes nothing but strife, But wisdom is with those who receive counsel.* Proverbs 13:10

The above verses come from the First Testament of the Bible. The Pharisee in the earlier parable was highly educated as to the First Testament. He knew the Proverbs in his head but did not know them in his heart. There is about a 14 inch distance from the head to the heart but for many it is a road that has not been traveled. Therefore, let us be humble like the tax collector and acknowledge our sins and shortcomings and that God is the One who supplies grace to overcome all sin and weakness. When Jesus said to Paul: *"...My grace is sufficient for you, for power is perfected in weakness." Paul was able to say: Most gladly, therefore, I will rather boast about my weaknesses, so that the power of Christ may dwell in me.* 2Corinthians 12:9

That word power is the same word that Jesus used: *...but you will receive power when the Holy Spirit has come upon you; and you shall be My witnesses both in Jerusalem, and in all Judea and Samaria, and even to the remotest part of the earth. And after He had said these things, He was lifted up while they were looking on, and a cloud received Him out of their sight.* Acts 1:8-9

It is clear that any grace or power that we receive is a gift from God that should always be humbly acknowledged. Pride is so insidious.

As the apostle John said: *For all that is in the world, the lust of the flesh and the lust of the eyes and the boastful pride of life, is not from the Father, but is from the world.* 1John 2:16 These three are the basic causes of all sin. The boastful pride of life is to trust in our own powers and presumption to trust in the stability of earthly things rather than in God.

Let's pray right now to the Lord to deliver us from all selfish pride!

Hmm, So You Have A Problem Workbook

Questions:

1. The world regards _____ as an attribute.
2. God regards _____ as a stumbling block or a detriment.
3. The word _____ in the Hebrew means arrogance, excellency, majesty pomp, swelling, to strut, haughtiness (as evinced by the attitude).
4. The word _____ in the Greek means to inflate with self conceit, high minded, to be lifted up with pride, haughtiness, appearing above others, conspicuous.
5. Peter said *Put on _____ because God sets Himself against proud ones, but he gives grace to humble ones.*
6. A very proud person usually feels he does not need _____.
7. The humble person sees himself as he is and in deep need of _____.
8. We stand by the _____ of God, not our own works.
9. The Pharisee knew scripture in his head, but not in his _____.
10. The apostle John said *the lust of the flesh, the lust of the eyes and boastful _____ of life is not from the Father but is from the world.*
11. What three things are the major causes of all the sin in the world. _____ _____ _____

Discuss the parable of the publican and the Pharisee and how pride and humility were seen by the Lord in them.

Hmm, So You Have A Problem Workbook

Chapter 21

ANGER CAN KILL

Certainly anger kills a stubborn fool... Job 5:2

What a statement! The angry Type A or irritable person is really hurting himself with his anger.

I was going on a trip with a friend, Ann, and I was telling her about my friend who was learning to play tennis. Her husband was extremely critical of her.

Ann told me this story. She married when she was 15. Her husband knew how to play tennis and was teaching her. If she didn't volley or serve the way he wanted her to, he hit her! I came home with this story to tell my friend that her husband was not all that bad after all!

Ann's husband died in an automobile accident when he was only 19. As I was relating the story to my husband, he said that Ann's husband's anger probably led to the accident. So as Eliphaz said: ... *anger kills a stubborn fool.....* Job 5:2

I don't think that there are many people in their seventies or eighties who are angry all the time. To live that long they must have become mellower, as anger is a killer. It can cause hypertension, heart attacks, high blood pressure, and various other medical problems. Think about it. Blood does not flow properly in an angry person. Their faces get red, their muscles become taut, and there is tremendous stress. All this takes its toll on the human body. We are not created to have tension in our systems. We are created to have peace.

Things said in anger cannot be reversed. Things done in anger are almost always regretted. No child learns well from an angry parent or teacher. As Eliphaz said, the angry person is a stubborn person, quick to take offense and slow to reason. The angry person may also be a lonely person because who wishes to associate with an angry person? So anger is not only detrimental to one's health, but also to one's social life. Paul the apostle said: *Don't get so angry that you sin.*

Hmm, So You Have A Problem Workbook

Don't go to bed angry and don't give the devil a chance. Ephesians 4:26-27

If we go to bed angry, by the next morning all things are out of proportion. After a while we are angry without a cause and may not even remember the original cause. If you are married, always kiss each other good night. Don't allow destructive anger to fester.

Righteous anger is acceptable and necessary. We can be angry against criminal acts and unrighteous deeds. However the Bible says not to be so angry that we sin. Let's consider the anger that infidelity produces. If a spouse is unfaithful in thought or deed, isn't that grounds for anger? Initially yes, but to hold the anger does nothing for the situation. It must be resolved, either by confession and forgiveness, or if it continues, I believe that separation is the answer.

I have a friend who is very close to the Lord. One night she couldn't fall asleep. She nudged her husband and asked him if he was thinking about another woman. He said yes. She told him to stop! Then she was able to go to sleep. Truly the woman lives in God's favor for not becoming angry.

The angry person is usually angry about things that pertain to him, not to unrighteous deeds committed to others. Excessive pride and self- centerness often accompany anger. If we are that angry person, we can humble ourselves before God, and ask Him to take away that negative emotion. Every time we start to get angry over foolish things, why not consider what it is doing to our bodies and our relationships with others? Anger usually precedes murder. So a person can get killed by excessive anger. Also a person can kill by excessive anger. Is it an emotion that needs to be nurtured? No! So let's leave it on the altar and ask God to quiet our natures down, so that we no longer are that angry person we were.

Note: If you are dealing with an angry person, please see the chapter "A Gentle Answer."

Hmm, So You Have A Problem Workbook

Questions:

1. Whom does anger hurt? _____
2. *Anger kills a _____ fool.*
3. _____ can cause hypertension, heart attacks, high blood pressure.
4. We are created to have _____ not anger.
5. An angry person is quick to take _____
6. Paul said *don't go to _____ angry.*
7. _____ usually precedes murder.
8. If we are an angry person, can we ask God to take it away? ____

Discuss how anger has led you to get into trouble.

Hmm, So You Have A Problem Workbook

Chapter 22

I DON'T GET MAD, I GET EVEN

Do not take revenge, dear friends, but leave room for God's wrath. For it is written, "Vengeance belongs to me. I will pay them back, declares the Lord." Romans 12:19

Let's consider the statement that we sometimes hear: "I don't get mad, I get even." We will see that the statement is an oxymoron - impossible to get even if we do not stay angry. How can we remember to get even when we are not angry? How much in life do we forget? So many things! What do we retain? Probably two emotions drive us to remember or retain - love and hatred.

My husband and I were in Egypt and traveling back to the states when a terrible sandstorm occurred. We were locked into security and had to wait until the storm subsided. Trying to sleep on the hard benches I closed my eyes thinking about my little grandchildren, how sweet and beautiful and what a gift they were. How much I loved them! Suddenly hearing a tap on the dividing window, I looked into the faces of some other sweet little children. They were from the Sudan and were traveling also. So I started to duck down and reappear - playing hide and seek. They were laughing and playing with me. Sweet memories of love. I'm smiling as I write this.

Now let's look at memories from anger or hurt. Why do we stay hurt about situations? Is it because we are angry? Think about it. Anger will keep us remembering painful situations. I once heard a lady say, "I distinctly remember forgetting that!" What a blessing it is to have made ourselves forget something that was painful.

If we hold on to that disappointment, sin, or hurt, guess what! We retain the sin and have to deal with it, over and over again. Consciously or subconsciously we go over and over that which was done to us, and it gets enlarged and hideous. Why do we see countries, for example, Yugoslavia, separating into Bosnia and Croatia and then slaughtering each other? Why are people in Ireland still killing each other? Could it be because they are unwilling to forgive the sins of their ancestors and thus keep the fuels of hatred burning?

Now, let's consider, do we ever get even? Tit for tat, bon chat, bon rat (good cat, good rat). It never ends! We have the power to end things by forgiveness. When we truly forgive, we will truly forget. Even if we see the person who hurt us, if we have truly forgiven, the past will not be dredged up and we will be free. Negative emotions do so much harm to our minds and bodies. I am convinced that many of our physical ailments are due to the stress of remembering bad things.

So, right now, can we pray to throw those negative things into a sea of forgetfulness and start off fresh again?

Hmm, So You Have A Problem Workbook

Questions:

1. To whom does vengeance belong? _____.
2. Probably two emotions _____ and _____ cause us to remember things.
3. It is impossible to get even without being _____.
4. It is a _____ to make ourselves forget something painful.
5. We have the power to end things by _____.
6. When we truly forgive, we truly _____.

Discuss how we threw negative emotions into the sea of forgetfulness.

Hmm, So You Have A Problem Workbook

Chapter 23

HATE CAN DESTROY

For the sorrow that is according to the will of God produces a repentance without regret, leading to salvation, but the sorrow of the world produces death. 2Corinthians 7:10

Is hate the opposite of love? More likely, indifference is the opposite of love. But hate is one of the strongest negative emotions that we can feel. It precedes slander, rape, fighting, and murder. We are not born to hate, so how does it arise in us? How does a child become hateful? Let's consider the above verse.

Sorrow according to the will of God. Do we see that the first emotion is sorrow? Why do we become sorrowful? Could it be because of lack of love? A person who is loved usually does not feel sorrow, but the person who is unloved probably will feel sorrow. In my years of teaching in the jails, I have seen so clearly the choices that people make when in a very hard, sorrowful state. Some will choose life - love and forgiveness - and others will choose death - hatred and bitterness. I have heard people say that hatred was deep inside of them, but after considering what Jesus had done for them, that hatred disappeared.

So we see that to hold onto hatred is a choice. We can realize that it was not born in us, but probably grew because of disappointments with loved ones. We can bring those disappointments to the cross of Jesus as He said to us: *"Come to Me, all who are weary and heavy-laden, and I will give you rest."* Matthew 11:28

Weary means over burdened. If we have hate in our hearts, it is a heavy burden. We become consumed with that emotion and have no rest. However, Jesus said He will give us rest to recover and collect ourselves if we will come unto Him. To collect ourselves - to return to sanity. To be consumed with hatred is not sane behavior. No rational human being desires to be consumed with such an emotion.

Paul said: *And so people become enemies of God when they are*

Hmm, So You Have A Problem Workbook

controlled by their human nature; for they do not obey God's law, and in fact they cannot obey it. Romans 8:7 We become enemies of God - there is hatred in our hearts - when we are controlled by our human nature. Only when we give ourselves over to God in repentance, can there be a change in our hearts.

So now we see that God's love is an antidote to hatred. We can always know that God will never betray our trust. As the writer of Hebrews said: *…be content with what you have, for God has said, "I will never leave you or abandon you." Hence we can confidently say, "The Lord is my helper; I will not be afraid. What can anyone do to me?"* Hebrews 13:5-6

How many times have we read about convicted murderers who have changed hearts after they receive Christ? Who does the changing? Jesus!

So now let's pray for forgiveness for all the sins we have committed and acknowledge that Jesus died for our sins and that He rose from the dead and He is God. Ask Him to come into your life as your Lord and Savior. If you pray this prayer sincerely, your life will change, hatred will lose its grip on you, and you will enter into the life that God has ordained for you to live.

Hmm, So You Have A Problem Workbook

Questions:

1. *For the sorrow that is according to the _____ of God produces a repentance without regret leading to salvation.*
2. *But the sorrow of the world produces _____.*
3. Is hate the opposite of love? _____
4. Most likely _____ is the opposite of love.
5. _____ can produce slander, rape, fighting, and murder.
6. We are not born to _____.
7. Considering what Jesus has done for us, should the _____ disappear at the cross? _____
8. Holding on to _____ is a choice.
9. Where can we bring all our burdens to? The _____.
10. Only by giving ourselves over to God in repentance, can there be a _____ in our hearts.
11. *Be_____ with what you have _____ ,* Jesus said *I will never leave you or abandon you.*

Discuss how the Lord has changed our hearts.

Hmm, So You Have A Problem Workbook

Chapter 24

CONTROL - THE SUFFOCATOR

So if the Son sets you free, you will be absolutely free. John 8:36

Have you ever heard about Jezebel? She was a wicked queen during the reign of her husband King Ahab, who was equally evil. Jezebel felt she had to be in control of everything. One day her husband spotted a field that was near to their land and asked the owner, Naboth, to sell the field to him. Naboth said he couldn't sell that which was deeded to him through family. When the king returned to the palace downhearted, Jezebel conspired against Naboth to have him killed. Then the king took over the field that Naboth had owned. Doesn't that sound like wars?

Wars are fought largely over lands or territories. During World War II, Germany and Japan wanted more land, so they invaded countries to occupy them. During the Vietnam War, North Vietnam wanted control over South Vietnam, so they invaded to occupy and control.

This is what the controlling person does. He will do anything legal or illegal to control or dominate another person, work situations, neighborhoods, or church and group activities. The controlling person is usually very negative and devious and will stop at nothing to have his way. The controlling mate will often be jealous and overly suspicious, demanding all of the other person's time and attention, and will maneuver situations so that he can always be in control.

As parents we have a responsibility to control our children when we are bringing them up, but we must relinquish that control when they are adults and must not exercise control over other adults either. The more freedom we give our spouses, families, or friends, the more they will want to be with us.

Have you heard of people who divorce their husbands because their husbands were working so much that they were almost never home? They probably won't see them much if they divorce them! If our spouses are not home very much, then shall we consider if the home environment we create is pleasant?

If your spouses have other interests such as sport activities or other social activities and you do not wish to participate, then by all means, encourage them to enjoy themselves.

God wants us to be the opposite of a controlling person. He is our Creator and He is the One Who should be in control of our lives. When we give up control to Him, He will banish those negative emotions from ourselves. When we realize that we have responsibility for our lives and our lives only, we will relinquish that strong control that we have exercised on others (unless it is over our young children). Think about it. Control is really pride, isn't it? We feel that we are the only ones who can accomplish anything, so we try to take control over situations.

Jesus said: *So if the Son sets you free, you will be absolutely free.* John 8:36 If Jesus sets us free, shouldn't we set others free? In a free situation, love can grow and be nurtured. In a controlling situation, love gets stifled and dies. The choice is ours. The only control that we should exercise is self control.

Let's pray now to be concerned only with our own self control and not try to control others.

Hmm, So You Have A Problem Workbook

Questions:

1. *So if the Son sets you _____, you will be absolutely ____.*
2. In the story of Jezebel and King ____, we see an illustration of the way countries fight wars by taking over illegally other people's properties.
3. The _____ person will do anything legal or illegal to control or dominate another person.
4. The _____ person usually is often jealous or overly suspicious, and will maneuver situations so that he is in control
5. If your spouse wishes to engage in other activities than you do, should you let them? _____
6. Who should be the ultimate controller of our lives? _____
7. When we give up _____ to Him, He will banish those negative emotions from ourselves.
8. Control is really _____.
9. Jesus said *So if the Son sets us _____* shouldn't we set others ____?
10. The only control we should exercise is _____ control.

Discuss situations where we felt we had to be in control and it hurt our relationships with others.

Hmm, So You Have A Problem Workbook

Chapter 25

A GENTLE ANSWER

A gentle answer turns away wrath... Proverbs 15:1

I have a friend who loves the Lord very much. She has a really sweet spirit. She is the kind of person around whom you feel better. We were on the beach one day and she had a crocheted beach bag. Her husband picked it up and there was sand in whatever he was getting out of the bag. He proceeded to berate her about the bag but she quietly looked at him and said in a soothing voice, "I'll buy another one tomorrow." He was speechless. What could he say when she agreed with him?

Solomon told us *A gentle response defuses anger, but a sharp tongue kindles a temper-fire.* Proverbs 15:1

The gentle response in the Hebrew means tender, weak, faint. So a quiet answer is not pretended, it is tender. We cannot pretend to be tender - either we are or we are not. So my friend's heart was tender toward her husband when he berated her for something so insignificant, and his wrath was turned away.

What might have happened had she answered him sharply, telling him to buy a bag if he didn't like the bag she had bought? They probably might still be angry about it. Every time they would get ready to go to the beach, probably her anger would stir up against him and probably his anger would stir up against her. It never ends! So next time someone is angry with us for no real reason, let us try to turn the other cheek, to give a gentle answer. In so doing, it will turn away their wrath.

Wrath in the Hebrew means anger, poison, hot displeasure, rage. Poison is such a powerful meaning of the word. Wrath will poison our relationships with others; will poison our happiness, our well being. Try to imagine how your body feels when you experience wrath. The area around your heart gets constricted and you feel very tense. Then try to imagine how your body feels when you experience peace.

Hmm, So You Have A Problem Workbook

Everything inside is relaxed and calm. What are we doing to ourselves when we allow ourselves to experience wrath? It is very unpleasant and we are probably shortening our life spans. Shall we consider what Solomon said *Kind words are good medicine, but deceitful words can really hurt.* Proverbs 15:4

The King James Version says *"perverseness therein is a breach in the spirit."* Perverseness means distortion, viciousness. A breach in the spirit is a fracture, ruin, breaking, crashing, hurt, vexation. So let's make a choice right now, what do we want, good medicine or bad? Easy choice. Let's tell ourselves that wrath is a ruin to our spirits, and we will not allow ourselves to indulge in it.

Let's pray right now to be able to react with kindness and gentleness, no matter what is said to us.

Hmm, So You Have A Problem Workbook

Questions:

1. Solomon told us *A _____ response defuses anger, but a sharp tongue kindles a temper fire.*
2. The gentle response means _____, _____, _____.
3. If so, a quiet answer is not _____.
4. When we hold on to anger, it _____ ends.
5. Wrath in the Hebrew means _____, _____, _____, _____.
6. It will _____ our relationships with others.
7. When we experience _____, we feel _____ and _____.
8. Solomon said _____ *words are good medicine.*

Discuss how hot situations have been simmered down by kind words.

Chapter 26

DUAL PERSONALITY- HOW PREVALENT

And when He had come to the other side into the country of the Gergesenes, two demon-possessed ones met Him, coming out of the tombs, exceedingly fierce, so that no one might pass by that way. Matthew 8:28

The other accounts of the Gergesene Demoniacs mention only one person! This is the first instance in the Bible of dual personality. When one is fully possessed by a demon, he is definitely two personalities, two different persons. One may appear to be perfectly normal; the other is, as the gospel said, exceedingly fierce - furious, difficult, dangerous. I am not referring to when a person becomes angry and acts out occasionally, but when there is a definite personality change. This may explain why some cruel, violent acts are done by seemingly calm, nice persons. Demon possession doesn't always show itself all the time. When Jesus commanded the demons to leave, He did not go through an elaborate exorcism, as Hollywood would have us think necessary; He just said "Go!"

Mark told us...*in My name they will cast out demons.* Mark 16:17 *Words of caution about casting out demons - When the unclean spirit goes out of a man, it passes through waterless places seeking rest, and not finding any, it says, 'I will return to my house from which I came.' And when it comes, it finds it swept and put in order. Then it goes and takes along seven other spirits more evil than itself, and they go in and live there; and the last state of that man becomes worse than the first.* Luke 11:24-26

If the person from whom the demon was cast out does not fill himself with the presence of the Lord, his last state will be seven times worse than his previous state. So the person must be willing to receive the Lord when the demons are cast out. One must be careful to bring the person to a saving knowledge of the Lord when taking control of the demon by the Word of God. This explains how Ashley Smith, the young lady from Atlanta who led an escaped murderer to the Lord while he held her captive, was able to subdue him. She spent time with him, talking about the Lord, encouraging him in the Lord, even serving him and making him pancakes. He apparently was delivered! Most likely he will stay delivered!

The second caution is that we as an instrument of the deliverance know the Lord. Please do not attempt to command evil spirits without the Lord. It could be quite dangerous. Consider this *But also some of the Jewish exorcists, who went from place to place, attempted to name over those who had the evil spirits the name of the Lord Jesus, saying, "I adjure you by Jesus whom Paul preaches." Seven sons of one Sceva, a Jewish chief priest, were doing this. And the evil spirit answered and said to them, "I recognize Jesus, and I know about Paul, but who are you?" And the man, in whom was the evil spirit, leaped on them and subdued all of them and overpowered them, so that they fled out of that house naked and wounded.* Acts 19:13-16

If you have the Holy Spirit, He will guide you, as He guided Ashley Smith. If you recognize a spirit in yourself that is not of God, by all means, tell it to "Go in the Name of Jesus." James said *Therefore, submit yourselves to God. Resist the devil, and he will run away from you.* James 4:7 Submit is to be under obedience. If we are obedient to God, we will not have problems in these areas, for He will guide us.

Paul said *Therefore if anyone is in Christ, he is a new creature; the old things passed away; behold, new things have come.* 2Corinthians 5:17 The old things, primeval things, of the first age have gone by. Some writers refer to the old man or nature and the new man or nature. I think they are seeing the same thing that there were two natures before being in Christ, some extremely violent as the Gergesene demoniac, some not so violent but just as lost.

David said *Draw me not away with the wicked, and with the workers of iniquity, who speak peace to their neighbors, yet evil is in their hearts.* Psalm 28:3 This verse shows us the dual nature of unregenerate men. They can speak peace and appear to be peaceful but evil, mischief, bad are in their hearts. Have you ever been shocked by the actions of a seemingly peaceful person? I have! That represents the nature of man as Jeremiah said *The heart is deceitful above all things, and desperately wicked; who can know it?* Jeremiah 17:9 However, there is an antidote to the wicked heart. John said *...that if our heart accuses us, we know that God is greater than our heart and knows all things. Beloved, if our heart does not accuse us, we have confidence toward God.* 1John 3:20-21

God is greater than our hearts! Even after we know the Lord and are walking in His ways, our hearts can accuse or condemn us for the life we lived before. But John said that God is greater than our hearts! He knows all things about us, but forgives all things and covers all things when we turn to Him for salvation and forgiveness. So we must not let the enemy accuse us of our past when we have put it behind us in salvation. God has forgiven us and we must forgive ourselves also.

Let's approach the throne of grace and ask the Lord for forgiveness for all the sins that we have committed and to cleanse our hearts in His love, grace, and forgiveness.

Hmm, So You Have A Problem Workbook

Questions:

1. What kind of personality did the Gergesene Demoniac have? _____
2. _____ possession does not always show itself all the time.
3. When Jesus said to the demon _____ it went.
4. Mark told us that Jesus said *in My* _____ *they will cast out demons.*
5. The story in Luke tells us that if a demon leaves a person and the person does not fill his heart with the Lord it will come back with ____ more.
6. So the person should be willing to fill his heart with _____.
7. We must also know the Lord as the _____ sons of Sceva found out when they tried to cast out demons in His name.
8. Who will guide us in the area? _____
9. *If our hearts accuse us,* _____ *is greater than our hearts.*
10. John said *if our heart does not* _____ *us, we have confidence toward God.*
11. Our hearts can _____ accuse us because of our past.
12. If God has forgiven us, should we continue to accuse ourselves for past sins? _____

Discuss if we or others we have encountered have had a dual personalty.

Chapter 27

LOVE IS NOT RECEIVING, IT IS GIVING

Love is patient, love is kind and is not jealous; love does not brag and is not arrogant, does not act unbecomingly... 1Corinthians 13:4-5

A major reason many marriages are failing is that people are looking for someone to love them, not for a person to whom they may give their love. There are books outlining the steps a man must make in courtship - calling for a date at least three days in advance, remembering special days, etc. Not often enough do the books delve into the true meaning of love.

Let's consider how God loves in order to determine the true meaning of love. It is an outright gift. The word for God's love in the Greek is agape which means affection or benevolence; specifically a love feast, dear; a feast if given by one person for others, especially a feast of charity. Throughout the Bible we see examples of God's giving.

Consider the life of Jesus. In all He did, He gave to others. He did not give to receive because it was His nature to give. The apostle James said *Every good and perfect gift comes down from the Father who created all the lights in the heavens. He is always the same and never makes dark shadows by changing.* James 1:17

Another example is Paul's great chapter on love - which is quoted at many marriage ceremonies: *Love is patient, love is kind and is not jealous; love does not brag and is not arrogant, does not act unbecomingly; it does not seek its own, is not provoked, does not take into account a wrong suffered, does not rejoice in unrighteousness, but rejoices with the truth; bears all things, believes all things, hopes all things, endures all things. Love never fails...* 1Corinthians 13:4-8

The word fail in the Greek means to drop away, specifically to be driven out of one's course; figuratively to lose, become inefficient; fall away; have no effect.

When we love someone, it has to take some effect. We may not see the result of our given love immediately, but it has taken place. Does this mean that everyone will respond to our love? Unfortunately, no. There are many people, because of the various problems discussed in this book, who are presently incapable of relating to another person. To maintain a relationship between two people, we must see a response to our love. However, we can be the person who gives it first.

If we are looking for someone to love us, we will always be disappointed. God gives us love and then we respond to Him. We don't initiate the emotion and then expect Him to respond. In the same way, we can love people first and then they may respond. If they do, it is a bonus. If they don't, let us not despair, we can continue to show love to others first.

Let's pray right now to be able to give to others the type of love that Jesus has given to us.

Hmm, So You Have A Problem Workbook

Questions:

1. _____ *is not receiving, it is* _____.
2. Why do many relationships fail? _____
3. God's love is an _____ gift.
4. In all Jesus did, He _____
5. 1Corinthians 13 the word _____ means to drop away, to lose.
6. When we love someone, it has to take some _____.
7. Does everyone respond to our love? _____
8. If we are looking for someone to love us, we may be _____

Discuss how we may have spurned someone's love or someone has spurned us and our reactions to the rebuff.

Hmm, So You Have A Problem Workbook

Chapter 28

HUSBANDS LOVE YOUR WIVES

Husbands love your wives. Ephesians 5:25

Paul did not say, "Wives love your husbands." Hmm, interesting! Why do you think Paul did not say for wives to love their husbands? Women are equal to but different from men. The first woman was created from a bone in Adam's rib: *The Lord God fashioned into a woman the rib which He had taken from the man, and brought her to the man. The man said, "This is now bone of my bones, And flesh of my flesh; She shall be called Woman, Because she was taken out of Man."* Genesis 2:22-23

So we see that woman was created from a bone from Adam's side, not from his foot, so we can conclude that women are on an equal basis with men. Paul said *There is neither Jew nor Greek, there is neither slave nor free man., there is neither male nor female; for you are all one in Christ Jesus.* Galatians 3:28

So let's explore as to why Paul said for husbands to love their wives. Women respond to love. They are created that way. Take the angriest, grouchiest, unhappiest woman and put a little baby in her arms and she will melt like butter. She will croon to the baby and rock him in her arms. The baby is a little package of love, right? So when husbands give their wives love, women are created to respond to that love.

In chapter five of Ephesians, Paul was explaining the relationship between a man and a woman. He used the analogy of Jesus and the church, how Jesus loves the church as it is His body, and how the church can love and respect the Lord. He said *Men ought to love their wives just as they love their own bodies.* Ephesians 5:28 And also: *A wife should put her husband first, as she does the Lord.* Ephesians 5:22 Put her husband first! That means to respect your husband, not to make fun of him or embarrass him in front of other people. Many things done in jest are really serious.

Hmm, So You Have A Problem Workbook

So the equation is simple. Husbands love your wives and they will respond with respect. Your lives will be fulfilled in the way that God wishes us to live. Isn't that easy?

Let's pray to be the spouse that God wishes us to be.

Hmm, So You Have A Problem Workbook

Questions:

1. Paul said _____ *love your wives.*
2. Women are _____ but _____ than men.
3. Paul says *...there is neither male nor female; for you are all* _____ *in Christ Jesus.*
4. Women respond to _____.
5. Paul said _____ *are to love their wives just as they love their own bodies.*
6. He also said *A* _____ *should put her husband first, as she does the Lord.*

Discuss how male and female may be equal but different in regards to love.

Chapter 29

OVERCOMING SEXUAL PROBLEMS

For you have been bought with a price: therefore glorify God in your body... 1Corinthians 6:20

God is so kind that He doesn't want us to sin because when we do, we hurt ourselves and other people. He wants us to "love our neighbors as ourselves" as love does not hurt us or other people.

When asked questions about the Bible's teaching on various sexual attitudes, it was apparent that it would be easy for me to write a paper because 99.9% of the women who attend my Bible studies at the county jail believe that the Bible is the Word of God and all that is in it is true. They do not always obey all that is in the Bible, but they know that it is the Word of God and it is God's love letter to us.

So let's approach the question of sexuality from God's written Word. *The Lord made a woman out of the rib. The Lord God brought her to the man, and the man exclaimed, "Here is someone like me! She is part of my body, my own flesh and bones. She came from me, a man. So I will name her Woman!" That's why a man will leave his own father and mother. He marries a woman, and the two of them become like one person.* Genesis 2:22-24

Let's examine what happens when we become one flesh. When we have sex with someone, we do become one flesh. If we then leave that person and go to another, we leave part of ourselves, especially emotionally, with that first person. If we continue to have multiple sexual partners, we become very physically and emotionally divided. So we see that God in His wisdom has established that we should have one partner, one marriage, man and woman together. Adam was not complete by himself, neither are we. So we are not asked of God to indulge in any sexual practices other than sex between a husband and wife.

As to the problem of lesbianism and homosexuality, let's examine the Scriptures again. The word homosexual is translated in Bible

Hmm, So You Have A Problem Workbook

translations written past the 1900's. The reason why the word is not used in older translations is that homosexuality is a term that Freud invented. Before his time, it was called sexual sin or sodomy. It was never considered a lifestyle or choice.

So God let these people go their own way. They did what they wanted to do, and their filthy thoughts made them do shameful things with their bodies. They gave up the truth about God for a lie, and they worshiped God's creation instead of God, who will be praised forever. Amen.

God let them follow their own evil desires. Women no longer wanted to have sex in a natural way, and they did things with each other that were not natural. Men behaved in the same way. They stopped wanting to have sex with women and had strong desires for sex with other men. They did shameful things with each other, and what has happened to them is punishment for their foolish deeds. Since these people refused even to think about God, he let their useless minds rule over them. That's why they do all sorts of indecent things. Romans 1:24-28

Thus when we see from God's Word that He warned us against sexual sin, we can approach His throne and ask Him for help in this matter. We clearly see from Scripture that God does not want us to violate our bodies. He wants us to be united sexually only with our husbands or wives. He never asks us to do anything that is impossible for us to do. He always gives us grace to do that which He has asked. He loves us so much that He does not want us to be hurt.

So now please pray this with me. Dear Lord Jesus, I want to do Your will. Please give me the grace to become the person you created me to be. Please help me with my thought life so that I will not be tempted to do those things that You do not wish me to do. Please give me Your friendship and love so that I do not have to search for friendship and love in relationships that are not of Your approval. Thank you Jesus.

Hmm, So You Have A Problem Workbook

Questions:

1. God is so kind that He doesn't want us to _____ because when we do we hurt ourselves and other people.
2. When we have sex with someone, biblically we become _____ flesh.
3. So if we continually have sex with multiple partners, we become _____.
4. So God's plan for us is to have one partner, one _____, man and woman together.
5. Who first invented the word _____?
6. Before that, what was it called? _____
7. Whom can we approach for help in this matter? _____
8. Does He ever ask us to do something that is impossible to do? __

Discuss how in love you have been able to help someone in this matter.

Hmm, So You Have A Problem Workbook

Chapter 30

WHY DO WE LIMIT GOD IN OUR LIVES?

O magnify the LORD with me, and let us exalt his name together. Psalm 34:3

Do we really comprehend God? I don't think so. If we look at the ocean, the animals, the sky, the trees, and most of all our human bodies that function so marvelously, why do we limit the God Who created us? Some people disdain those who believe in miracles, healings, and manifestations of the presence of God. Why do we not believe when we can see the wonders of God all around us! Every leaf on a tree is different, every snowflake and every person. If God can create such diversity in natural things, why couldn't He perform other miracles such as healing?

The Psalmist said magnify - to make large, as in body, mind, estate, honor. We tend to want to bring God down to our level rather than aspiring upward to His. When the realization hits us that "God is God!" we will treat Him with the respect due Him. Just because He allows us to be friends with Him does not mean that we are equal to Him. We are created beings and will always be created beings.

Lucifer (satan's name when he was an archangel in Heaven) wanted to ascend higher than God. He lost sight of the fact that he was a created being, not a god. God spoke to him saying: *How you are fallen from the heavens, O shining star, son of the morning! How you are cut down to the ground, you who weakened the nations! For you have said in your heart, I will go up to the heavens, I will exalt my throne above the stars of God; I will also sit on the mount of the congregation, in the sides of the north. I will go up above the heights of the clouds; I will be like the Most High. Yet you shall be brought down to hell, to the sides of the Pit.* Isaiah 14:12-15

Thus we see that the one who denied magnifying God and proudly wanted to be like God has been thrown out of Heaven. He was sent crashing down to Hades where he seeks to do whatever he can do to us. He also took one-third of the angels with him and he is very crafty and persuasive.

One day, I was bothered by some individuals' behavior toward me and I was thinking about resentments. Early in the evening, I knew that I had to go to the cross (the teacher always has to apply what he/she has taught!) so I read the Passion of Jesus in the book of John. Jesus said just before He died, *"It is finished."* John 19:30 So right at that time I prayed and my whole attitude changed. Everything was lifted. I had been limiting God in my life! This is God's promise: *Therefore, submit yourselves to God. Resist the devil, and he will run away from you.* James 4:7 So why limit God in our lives when we can be magnifying Him?

Let's pray right now that we will never limit God in our lives again.

Hmm, So You Have A Problem Workbook

Questions:

1. Do we really comprehend God? _____
2. Can we limit God? _____
3. What does magnify mean in the bible? _____

4. Lucifer (satan's name when he was an archangel) lost sight of the fact that he was a _____ being, not a creator.
5. Jesus said just before He died *It is* _____.
6. If God's promise is that it is finished, can He solve any problem? _____

Discuss how in some ways you have limited God in your lives.

Chapter 31

IS YOUR FAITH REAL?

...the Spirit of God came upon him also, so that he went along prophesying continually... 1Samuel 19:23

We know that King Saul was not a prophet, but when he was among a great company of prophets, he prophesied also. The people wondered about this. Do you feel the presence of the Lord when you are in a group setting such as church but fail to feel His presence when alone? Some of us, like King Saul, may be riding on the faith and holiness of others.

Jesus talked about that in Matthew chapter 25 verses 1-12 when He told us about the 10 virgins. They all looked similar and dressed alike, but when the bridegroom summoned them, five did not have oil in their lamps. Oil signifies the presence of the Holy Spirit. Paul told us 1Corinthians 12:3 *Therefore, only by the Holy Spirit can we know that Jesus is Lord.*

We should examine ourselves and pray to the Lord that He will make Himself real to us. We cannot be filled with the Holy Spirit just because our parents or spouses have a deep relationship with the Lord. The writer of Hebrews said *Let us have confidence, then, and approach God's throne, where there is grace. There we will receive mercy and find grace to help us just when we need it.* Hebrews 4:16 So each of us can approach the throne of grace for a personal relationship with the Lord. Let's not be content with a superficial one. What Jesus wants from us is the relationship that a husband and wife should have - a deep knowing bond with no reservations.

I asked the women in the county jail who were in my Bible study how often they attended religious services during the week. Most of them said about five times. Then I asked them how often they attended when they were released. Almost all said never. So no wonder they often return to jail. I exhorted them to find a good church and become active at that church, read the Bible every day and pray every day.

Hmm, So You Have A Problem Workbook

The women that I have seen being successful when freed from jail are the ones who stay in a close relationship with Jesus. They are developing their own real relationship with Him, not relying upon someone else who has the presence of the Lord.

Paul said...*for all have sinned and fall short of the glory of God*. Romans 3:23 Yes, we all have sinned. However, the question arises, if we know Jesus and have faith in Him, are we continuing to sin? Have we really been redeemed when we continue in sin? If we do sin, we should repent immediately. Otherwise shall we question our faith in God? When David had seriously sinned with Bath Sheba and the prophet Nathan had revealed his sin to him, David said, *"Restore unto me the joy of thy salvation."* Psalm 51:12 He had lost the joy of his salvation and had not realized it! So if we do not have the joy that we had when we first came to the Lord, we can pray that the Lord will *increase our faith* Luke 17:5 as the apostles asked Jesus to do for them.

If we have once felt the presence of the Lord and felt close to Him and now have drifted away, shall we ask ourselves if any little sins have driven us away? Solomon said *Catch the foxes for us, The little foxes that are ruining the vineyards...* Song of Solomon 2:15

Small sins that are not addressed can make us drift away from the Lord. When our conscience bothers us even about small things, we must immediately stop and consider. Usually people drift away from the Lord by small sins, rather than by some huge transgressions.

Each of us must develop a personal relationship with Jesus. And we can do that by studying our Bibles, praying to the Lord, and waiting on Him to fill us with His presence.

Let's pray right now that we will be filled with the Holy Spirit and we will always keep the sweet presence of the Lord.

Hmm, So You Have A Problem Workbook

Questions:

1. Who prophesied in the company of other prophets but was not a prophet? _____
2. If we only feel God's presence when in the company of others but not alone, may we be riding on the faith and holiness of others?___
3. Only by the _____ _____ can we say that Jesus is Lord.
4. If we do not pray, read our bibles, stay in the presence of the Lord we may _____.
5. If we truly are saved, should we continue to sin? _____
6. King _____ was sinning but did not realize it until the prophet Nathan brought him into a realization of it.
7. _____ sins not addressed can lead us to _____ sins.

Discuss how each of us may develop our own personal relationship with Jesus.

Hmm, So You Have A Problem Workbook

Chapter 32

AM I DOING GOD A FAVOR?

"I am the LORD, and I do not change." Malachi 3:6

If I get up early and spend time with the Lord, am I doing God a favor? If I pray longer today than I usually pray, am I doing God a favor? NO! I am doing myself a favor. Is God the same if I pray or spend more time with Him? Yes! But am I the same if I spend more time with Him? NO! I am the one who is changed when I am in His presence. I am the one who is different when I sit at His feet for a longer time. Was Jesus the same when the people were thronging at his side or did He change when He was alone at Gethsemane? He was the same! We are the ones who change.

Sometimes we think that God needs us, but we are the ones who really need Him. We may, however, please Him by being in His presence. Zephaniah told us that *He will joy over thee with singing.* Zephaniah 3:17

Perhaps the feeling of doing God a favor comes from the old religious thinking of doing sacrifices to please God. He paid it all at the cross, the whole price for our salvation. There is nothing we can do to save ourselves. When we realize God's grace in His sacrifice for our salvation, our thinking will change.

Paul said *But God demonstrates His own love toward us, in that while we were yet sinners, Christ died for us.* Romans 5:8 While we were yet sinners! There is nothing that we could do to make God save us, He did it all. It is a completely free gift from Him! And when we realize that, we will repent because we will see ourselves as we are and feel sorrow for the life we have led and wish to beg forgiveness from God for being such a sinner. Did we rob banks, kill people, or commit fraud? Maybe not, but if we told a lie when we were twelve years old or had mean thoughts about our parents, we are still sinners. When we clearly see ourselves as we are, not the person we were in our own minds, the tears of repentance will flow.

Hmm, So You Have A Problem Workbook

What part did we play in being born? None! And the same analogy is true about the part we play in being born again. Jesus told Nicodemus ...*Most positively, I say to you, unless someone is born from above [or, born again], he is not able to see the kingdom of God.* John 3:3 *so that every [one] believing [or, trusting] in Him shall not perish, but shall be having eternal life.* John 3:15 Jesus did not outline steps for Nicodemus to take to enter the kingdom of God, He said whoever believes in Him will have eternal life. He is looking for faith, not works. If we have faith, works will follow, but works do not bring us into the kingdom of God, into salvation. Faith in Jesus that He is God and has redeemed us will bring us there. How do we appropriate that faith? We receive it from Him. It is an outright gift. We just open our hands and hearts to Him and ask Him to live in us.

Jesus said *"I am the way, the truth, and the life; no one goes to the Father except by me."* John 14:6 Jesus is the way we come to the Father. He is the truth and He is the life, the new life we live when we invite Him in our hearts.

So shall we pray now to invite Jesus to come into our hearts and live there forever.

Hmm, So You Have A Problem Workbook

Questions:

1. Whom do I do a favor to if I spend more time with the Lord and pray more? _____
2. Who is changed when I spend more time in His presence? _____
3. Zephaniah said that *He will* _____ *over you with singing.*
4. So can we bring joy to the Lord? _____
5. Salvation is a _____ gift from God.
6. Jesus told Nicodemus *Unless someone is* _____ *from above, he is not able to see the kingdom of God.*
7. If we have faith, _____ will follow.

Discuss the glorious time when you were born again.

Chapter 33

ADOPTION- PERHAPS THE BEST MOTHERS

Hannah made a solemn promise: "Lord Almighty, look at me, your servant! See my trouble and remember me! Don't forget me! If you give me a son, I promise that I will dedicate him to you for his whole life ..." 1Samuel 1:11

I have two friends who were adopted. One was a neighbor and the other a close friend. They both are the nicest women that I know. My neighbor, who lived on a farm nearby, told me her story before she died. Her mother was Canadian and she asked farmers in New Hampshire to watch her child (this was back in the 1920s) for a while when she went back to Canada. So the farmers took in the little child but the mother never returned. The farmers brought up my friend as their own child. She was gentle and sweet, always smiling and pleasant and there to take care of her parents until they died.

An older Italian family adopted my other friend, who had been a red haired, freckled Irish child. They doted on her. When she was in her sixties and her adoptive parents had died, she looked up her birth parents. Her biological mother and father had come together to Boston from Ireland and they were very poor. They couldn't afford to bring up another child. When my friend's adoptive mother was ill, she was the one who took loving care of her until she died. These are two great success stories about adoption.

The Bible has another success story! Have you heard of the prophet Samuel? He was one of the greatest men of God in the First Testament. His mother Hannah was barren for very much a long time. Her husband loved her a lot. He tried to console her, but her heart yearned for a child. One day when they were on their annual pilgrimage to the temple, she was praying so hard for a child that the priest Eli thought she was drunk. When he chided her she told him her story. He promised her that next year at this time she would have a child.

Hmm, So You Have A Problem Workbook

The next year she bore Samuel. She remembered her promise to the Lord to dedicate her child to Him. After she had weaned him, she brought Samuel up to the temple to live with Eli. The Bible doesn't say how long she breast fed him, but I think it might have been quite a while. It would have been for me if I were to dedicate my only child and just see him once a year. Samuel later became one of the greatest prophets. He heard directly from the Lord in an audible voice when he was only a young lad and he did all that the Lord required.

Perhaps if Hannah had kept her son he might have grown up to be a nice man, married, with children, but he would never have been in a position to be the high priest of Israel. The people of Israel had not had a good prophet over them for a long time. Hannah's sacrifice probably changed the course of history.

I was counseling a sweet lady who was in the county jail who was pregnant. She asked me about adoption, and I encouraged her. She had a 10 year old son in the mid west, where she was going to relocate. Also her uncle had promised her a job. She was ready to start her life again.

A couple who lived nearby was trying to adopt a child. The wife had had a hysterectomy and couldn't have any more children and she desperately wanted one more. So now she and her husband are bringing up my friend's child and my friend is able to rebuild her life again.

The mothers who give their children up for adoption are really unselfish mothers as they are seeking a future for their children, not just the immediate satisfaction of keeping them. It is difficult to give up children, but so many grow up in safe and loving environments when their mothers truly look to their future. If you are contemplating adoption, you may call 1-800-Bethany. This is a national adoption agency, and its reputation is excellent. Let's pray now for wisdom concerning adoption.

Hmm, So You Have A Problem Workbook

Questions:

1. The bible has a success story about _____ and her child _____

2. Do you think if she had not kept her promise to the Lord he would not have been the great leader he was? _____

3. The mothers or fathers who give their children up for adoption are really _____.

4. Is it unselfish to provide for your children when you are unable to? _____

Discuss situations where one needs wisdom in this area.

EPILOGUE – TYING IT ALL TOGETHER

If we do not neutralize at the Cross every negative emotion that we receive, we probably will transfer it to another person. Think about it. If we are rejected as a child, we may reject our spouse by infidelity, or we may reject our children by not being able to love them to the extent they need. The person who is an alcoholic or drug addict very often has children who are also addictive. But we don't have to continue in such a life - Jesus took it all at the Cross!

So if we suffer in any way, all we should do is turn to Jesus and He will carry our burdens for us. He acts exactly opposite to the way of the world. He was beaten and crucified because of the evil we did and would do, and yet we are healed by His sacrifice. We are forgiven at the Cross and the curse of sin is broken there. How deeply Jesus negated the original sin of Adam and Eve with His suffering.

He gives us His joy for our sadness, love for our rejection, health for our sicknesses, love for our anger, and joy for our depression and anxiety! What a swap! Why do we suffer another minute in these negative states?

Jesus said *"Come to Me, all who are weary and heavy-laden, and I will give you rest. Take My yoke upon you and learn from Me, for I am gentle and humble in heart, and you will find rest for your souls. For My yoke is easy and My burden is light."* Matthew 11:28-30

With Jesus, we can trade our burdens and labors for a high life in Him if we humble ourselves, admit our sins, repent of and turn from our sins, and accept Him as Lord and Savior. How can we resist such a glorious trade? How can we wish to continue in a life filled with sorrow and despair when He offers us such a life!

Let's pray earnestly for God to come into our lives now.

Hmm, So You Have A Problem Workbook

Questions:

1. If we do not neutralize at the Cross every negative emotion that we have received we probably will transfer it to _____.
2. If we are _____ as a child, we may _____ our spouses by infidelity.
3. Also we may _____ our children as we were _____.
4. Who took all these problems to the cross? _____
5. And to whom can we turn to carry our burdens? _____
6. Where is the curse of sin broken? _____
7. He gives us _____ for sadness, _____ for rejection, _____ for sicknesses, _____ for anger, _____ for depression.
8. With Him, we can trade our burdens for a _____ life in Him.

Discuss how we have taken our burdens to the Cross and how He has given us a high life in Him.

Hmm, So You Have A Problem Workbook

www.ingramcontent.com/pod-product-compliance
Lightning Source LLC
LaVergne TN
LVHW080041090426
835510LV00041B/1893